PRODUCT-LED GROWTH

How to Build a Product That Sells Itself

Author Bio

Wes Bush is a challenger. He's challenged himself by running marathons, skydiving, and building a remote business. He's challenged an entire industry to find a better way to approach SaaS growth. Wes is allergic to the status quo.

As founder and president of the Product-Led Institute, Wes spends his days teaching SaaS businesses how to flip the traditional sales playbook and ignite their growth engine with the Product-Led Growth methodology.

Wes holds a Bachelor's Degree in Global Business and Digital Arts from the University of Waterloo. A respected business consultant, Wes understands that flashy marketing and hard sells can't replace the value a customer receives from an exceptional product.

A strong brand and social proof are no longer enough to build trust with the modern buyer. People need to try before they buy. Product-Led Growth turns that philosophy into an executable business strategy.

Learn more about the Product-Led Institute at ProductLed.com.

Praise For
Product-Led Growth

"The future of growth belongs to product-led companies. At HubSpot, we realized this a few years ago, which is why we disrupted our own business model before anyone else could."

- Kieran Flanagan, VP of Marketing, HubSpot

"Product-Led Growth is about helping your customers experience the ongoing value your product provides. It is a critical step in successful product design and this book shows you how it's done."

- Nir Eyal, Wall Street Journal Bestselling Author of "Hooked: How to Build Habit-Forming Products

"The future of growth is product led. Data shows that companies leveraging a Product-Led Growth strategy perform better on average – faster growth, higher margins, lower burn and stronger valuation multiples. Product-Led Growth will soon become the norm, making it table stakes for SaaS companies that want to win in their markets. What is your company doing to adapt to the product led growth revolution?"

– Blake Bartlett, Partner, OpenView

"Product-Led Growth changes how companies grow because it brings a focus on how the product you've built can help you acquire more customers. Customer acquisition doesn't just become something marketing is focused on, the responsibilities for acquiring great customers expands to the product team as well."

- Hiten Shah, Co-Founder of FYI, Product Habits and Crazy Egg

"Product-Led Growth might be buzz-wordy right now but this is going to just be called "good business" very soon."

- Val Geiser, Digital Strategist

"In a world where brands promise more than they can deliver, companies that embrace Product-Led Growth stand out from the pack. Promising a better life to our buyer is now table stakes. We need to deliver on that promise. Our customers deserve it. Instead of hiding our product behind closed doors - it's time to lead with our product and let people see for themselves if we deliver on our promise."

- Shobhit Chugh, Product Manager for Crashlytics, Google

"Product-Led Growth is about prioritizing the user experience in everything you do: your product, pricing, marketing, customer engagement and even buying experience. An incredible user experience inevitably leads to faster growth, greater customer expansion and best-in-class retention."

- Kyle Poyar, VP of Market Strategy, Openview

"Organizations that adopt product-led strategies don't just have higher customer satisfaction ratings, they scale faster all while spending a fraction on acquisition when compared to traditional sales-led organizations. Product is now the single biggest lever for growth - if you're not already moving in this direction, watch out."

- Jackson Noel, CEO, Appcues

"Product-Led Growth is the only distribution model worth undertaking once the market is mature."

-Pankaj Prasad, Director of Product Management, Salesforce

"Many SaaS businesses strive for $0 customer acquisition cost (CAC) and yet most still end up spending a small fortune acquiring each new customer. If you want to get to $0 CAC, Product-Led Growth is the only way you're going to make it happen."

- Olof Mathé, CEO, MixMax

"Product-Led Growth is the multiplier on top of all the marketing every company is already doing. If you're advertising without a product that naturally markets itself you might as well be lighting your cash on fire."

- Amar Ghose, CEO, ZenMaid

"Product-Led Growth means that every team in your business influences the product. Your marketing team will ask, "how can our product generate a demand flywheel." Your sales team will ask, "how can we use the product to qualify our prospects for us?." Your customer success team asks, "how can we create a product that helps customers become successful beyond our dreams?." By having every team focused on the product, you create a culture that is built around enduring customer value."

- Allan Wille, Co-Founder & CEO, Klipfolio

"From a marketing and sales perspective, Product-Led Growth is a game-changer. It means you can deliver on your promise to prospects. It also means the product sells itself if you get in front of people at the right stage of the buying process. Rather than stuffing leads into a leaky funnel, you are retaining happy customers who spread the word to others."

- Juliana Casale, Head of Marketing, CrazyEgg

"Product-Led Growth is about using your product and your product data to convert prospects, retain users and expand customers. In today's highly competitive SaaS market, Product-Led Growth needs to be an essential component of your technology business."

- Eric Boduch, Chief Evangelist, Pendo

"A strong brand and social proof are no longer enough to build trust with the modern buyer. You need to let people try before they buy. The Product-Led Growth model is how you make this whole approach to doing business a reality."

- Karim Zuhri, Head of Product Marketing, SafetyCulture

"At heart, Product-Led Growth is incredibly intuitive. It's understanding that no amount of flashy marketing or hard selling can replace the value a customer receives from a product built to fit their needs. Make something that consistently provides value and you can rely on your customers to come back again and again."

- Kristen DeCosta, Growth Marketer, Churn Buster

"The sales-led way of buying software: Read about the software, create a list of features needed, let sales qualify you, do a demo, and twist their arm so they give you a trial.

The product-led way of buying software: Just start using the product. Ask for help if you get stuck. Based on your usage and profile, receive personalized recommendations.

Which sounds better to you as a buyer?"

- Peter Caputa IV, CEO, Databox

"Given the low-barrier to entry in SaaS, competition has never been more fierce. To stand out from the crowd, you need a competitive advantage. Product-Led Growth is the one way to build a sustainable business while lowering your customer acquisition costs and churn."

- Anumita Bhargava, Digital Marketing Specialist, Altina

"Product Led Growth is a powerful framework, taking the best parts of product development and go to market expertise to build a customer-obsessed and fast-growing business. Putting your customer at the center of the experience helps you tap into their motivations and behaviors, building loyalty and driving revenue!"

- Francesca Krihely, Director of Growth Marketing, MongoDB

"Understanding Product-Led Growth is more than just understanding a new business philosophy...it's about empowering yourself to craft a strategy that will result in a better ROI for you and your business. Because in a Product-Led Growth world, your product sells itself and has the self-service levers to make that happen without needing to invest a fortune in sales and marketing."

- Matt Bilotti, Product Manager, Growth, Drift

"Product-Led Growth is the next evolution of software. Just look at the mobile apps market. Companies like Fortnite have made over a billion in revenue by using a freemium model where you simply pay for upgrades. By eliminating all barriers for someone to try the product and get value from using it, their product sells itself. Product-Led Growth is simply how you make this approach to doing business a reality."

- Justin McGill, CEO, LeadFuze

"At Tettra, we believe in growing our business via a product our customers use daily. Too often, VC-backed companies grow in an unsustainable way, forcing sales of a sub-optimal product. Instead, with a Product-Led Growth strategy, our growth is fueled by the value we bring to our customers every single day."

- Kristen Craft, Chief Revenue Officer, Tettra

"Product-Led Growth isn't a tactic or hack. It's a model that drives teams and companies to deliver the maximum value and experience to their customers directly from the products they build and design. Getting this right means you need a deep understanding of those you serve and how to help each customer become successful. If you can just get these two things right, you'll increase your odds of building a company with legacy value."

- David Axler, Growth and Business Development, WaveHQ

"I love Product-Led Growth because it's the only way to scale your growth without dramatically increasing your resources. You're using the product to sell itself which is the easiest kind of sell."

- Jennifer Stoldt, Head of Online Growth, Checkfront

"In our experience, a growth at all costs mentality distracts you from what's really important - helping your customers become successful. As a SaaS company, Product-Led Growth gives you a laser-focus on satisfaction and retention in order to build a sustainable business in the long run."

- David Roch, Head of Product, Marketgoo

"The way to achieve sustainable, recurring growth is not through sales, but through the product. At Lightning AI, we embraced Product-Led Growth and have been able to increase our activation rates by 164% when onboarding new users."

- Colette Nataf, CEO, Lightning AI

Contents

Introduction

History tells us that "how" you sell is just as important as "what" you sell. Just like Blockbuster couldn't compete with Netflix by selling the same digital content, you need to decide "when" not "if" you'll need to innovate on the way you sell.

One of the main reasons I decided to write this book was because I witnessed first-hand the power of Product-Led Growth. It all started in a cold, gusty winter in Waterloo, Ontario (a.k.a. the tech capital of Canada). In one cozy loft, over 50 hard workers plugged away on their laptops side-by-side on long plywood tables. Everyone was passionate about video.

Inside this startup, it was common for everyone to use video to communicate with their family, friends, co-workers, customers, and even prospects. At the time, this behavior was considered a bit weird, but video was quickly becoming a thing for businesses around the world—it was an exciting time. As a result, smart investors wanted to pour money into video companies to accelerate their growth and ride the wave of demand.

Since gaining access to capital wasn't an issue for this software company, the team was "blessed" with the opportunity to put some serious marketing firepower into promoting its new video hosting technology to the masses.

I was one of those marketers. I spent a small fortune on countless acquisition channels. I was laser-focused on generating leads. But after spending a stupid amount of cash, I began asking some hard "Whys" about customer acquisition—like why did I invest $300,000 promoting a whitepaper?

Obviously, the outcome was to generate leads for a hungry sales team. But why a whitepaper in the first place? We were using the same-old marketing playbook that everyone else did: Create content; use landing pages to capture leads; and nurture those leads with automated emails until, one day, they converted into paying customers (or unsubscribed). Sound familiar?

It wasn't until I helped launch a freemium product that soared to over 100,000 users in less than a year that I realized something was wrong with the old marketing playbook. By making it easy for people to experience the value of our product, we transformed it into a powerful customer acquisition model.

This one experience reinforced something I have long believed: **Truly great software companies are built to be product-led.** You don't have to be a genius to come to this conclusion. In our day-to-day lives, we expect to try products before we buy them. Whether you're contemplating perfume, a new shirt, or even a pair of sunglasses—you want to try it before you buy.

Trying a product is and always will be an essential part of the buying process. When it comes to software, consumers demand the same experience. Companies that embrace Product-Led Growth align their business model with an undeniable consumer trend that is not going anywhere.

As the SaaS industry evolves, I believe there will be two types of companies:

1. **Sales-led companies** represent the old way. It's complex, unnecessary, expensive, and all about telling consumers how the product will benefit them. These companies want to take you from Point A to Point B in their sales cycle.

2. **Product-led companies** flip the traditional sales model on its head. Instead of helping buyers go through a long, drawn-out sales cycle, they give the buyer the "keys" to their product. The company, in turn, focuses on helping the buyer improve *their life*. Upgrading to a paid plan becomes a no-brainer.

Today, a strong brand and social proof are no longer enough to build trust with the modern buyer. You need to let people try before they buy. Product-Led Growth is how you turn that approach into an executable business strategy.

To sell to the modern buyer, you need to decide: Are you going to be product-led? Or will you be disrupted?

Part I

Design Your Strategy

CHAPTER 1

Why Is Product-Led Growth of Rising Importance?

First off, what the heck is Product-Led Growth? Initially coined by OpenView, Product-Led Growth is a go-to-market strategy that relies on using your product as the main vehicle to acquire, activate, and retain customers.

If you've used Slack or Dropbox, you've witnessed this first-hand—you didn't read a lengthy whitepaper on the benefits of strong internal communication or cloud-based file sharing. You wanted to see the product in action!

On the surface-level, Product-Led Growth may look like a simple model for your buyer to **try before they buy.**

However, if we look deeper, Product-Led Growth is a

completely new way of growing a SaaS business.

As Allan Wille, Co-Founder & CEO, Klipfolio puts it:

> Product-Led Growth means that every team in your business influences the product. Your marketing team will ask, how can our product generate a demand flywheel. Your sales team will ask, how can we use the product to qualify our prospects for us? Your customer success team asks, how can we create a product that helps customers become successful beyond our dreams? By having every team focused on the product, you create a culture that is built around enduring customer value.

By leading with the product throughout an organization, product-led companies often benefit from shorter sales cycles, lower Customer Acquisition Costs (CAC) and a higher Revenue Per Employee (RPE).

Product-Led Growth isn't just about disrupting "how" SaaS companies sell, it's how you survive. Right now, a tsunami is coming to wipe out thousands of SaaS companies.

In this chapter, I'll walk you through the three tidal waves coming ashore and show you how to avoid their potentially disastrous consequences.

The Three Tidal Waves Coming for Your Subscription Business

Tidal Wave 1: Startups are more expensive to grow.

In one sense, this is counterintuitive: It has never been cheaper to build a SaaS company. (HackerNoon even goes so far as to claim that you can now build a SaaS product with $0.)[1]

However, because of this low barrier to entry, there's no shortage of competition. As a result, argues Andrew Chen,[2] it's becoming more expensive to acquire customers. Just take a look at these three channels:

- **Facebook:** 171% Increase in Cost per Thousand Impressions, or CPM;[3]

- **Twitter:** 20% Increase in CPM;[4]

- **LinkedIn:** 44% Increase in CPM.[5]

There are other channels, of course, but these numbers hint that, well, marketing isn't getting any cheaper. According to ProfitWell,[6] CACs have increased by over 55% in the last five years. During that same period, customer willingness to pay for features has dropped by 30%.

So, on one hand, we have rising costs; on the other, we have a lower willingness to pay. You don't have to be a financial whiz to understand that this means your expenses go up while your profitability goes down.

If you have high churn in your business, this tidal wave may be lethal. Wouldn't you agree?

Tidal Wave 2: Buyers now prefer to self-educate.

This isn't limited to the Business to Consumer (B2C) space. Three out of every four Business to Business (B2B) buyers would rather self-educate than learn about a product from a sales representative, according to Forrester.[7]

Let me ask you two questions:

1. Would you like to see and use a software product before buying it?

2. Or would you prefer to go through a lengthy sales process to see if it's a good fit?

If you're like most people, you'll opt for trying out the product on your own. This doesn't apply just to small and mid-size businesses. As Gainsight notes,[8] "Enterprise buyers also expect to try and evaluate software in an easy, frictionless way."

Trying out a product through a free-trial or freemium model[9] is less hassle and can help you decide quickly on a product.

Tidal Wave 3: Product experiences have become an essential part of the buying process.

If you've used Netflix, you've witnessed this first-hand—you didn't need to reach out to a sales rep or book a demo before you were able to watch and eventually buy the service. The entire onboarding and upgrade experience was handled by the product.

No need for human intervention. Now, that's not to say that product-led companies don't need sales reps. But your product needs to do the heavy lifting when it comes to getting new users up to speed.

These tidal waves aren't stopping anytime soon. They're here to stay. Consumers (like us) demand it. Your SaaS business might be able to weather *one* of these tidal waves, but do you really want to take a chance on surviving all three?

To put your SaaS business in the best position to win, you need to pick a go-to-market strategy that will place your business on high ground.

How to Put Your Subscription Business on High Ground

First off, what is a go-to-market strategy? **A** go-to-market (GTM) strategy[10] **is an action plan that specifies how a company will reach target customers and achieve a competitive advantage.**

Before we dive into which GTM strategies might work best for your business, you need to understand your market conditions, competitive positioning, ideal customer, and product offering.

Knowing each of these elements will help you choose a GTM strategy that will acquire, retain, and grow your customer base in the most capital-efficient way. Other strategies, in contrast, are ripe for disruption and put you at risk.

Why the Sales-Led Go-to-Market Strategy Is at Risk

If the only way you can sell a product is if someone talks to you, you're using a sales-led strategy. Even if you have a marketing engine that generates thousands of leads for your sales team, you're not off the hook.

This is because relying on your sales team to make every sale prevents you from helping your users self-educate. Whether you know it or not, you are adding an incredible amount of friction to the entire buying process. It also keeps your CACs high—great sales teams aren't cheap.

As you can see in the graph below, a sales-led GTM strategy puts you at risk for each tsunami wave.

1. The Sales-Led GTM Strategy

Tidal Waves	Safety Zone
Tidal Wave 1 – Self-Educate	✗
Tidal Wave 2 – Rising Acquisition Costs	✗
Tidal Wave 3 – Product Experience	✗

Even while being at risk of each wave, these are some reasons why you still might consider using a sales-led GTM:

Pros of a sales-led go-to-market strategy

1. Ability to close high Lifetime Value (LTV) customers.

A main lure of a sales-led GTM is that you can close customers with a high Annual Contract Value (ACV). This sounds great but can often lead to poor revenue diversity, with several customers making up a large percentage of your Annual Recurring Revenue (ARR).

If a single customer leaves, it could ruin your revenue projections and force you to unexpectedly lay off your employees. That said, if you're tackling enterprise first and have a highly complex solution, you may need a high-touch sales model because of the complexities of their procurement process and implementation.

2. Perfect for hyper-niche solutions.

If you have a product with a small Total Addressable Market (TAM), it often makes sense to forgo a product-led model in favor of a sales-led model. One of the biggest reasons is because the quality of the relationships you have with your market will have an outsized impact on how you grow your business. In contrast, the product-led model is built for a large TAM where you can scale rapidly.

3. Perfect for new categories.

When you're launching a new category, you have to change the way people approach problems. This not only takes time but requires you to educate people on how to do things differently.

As a result, it often makes sense to start with a sales-led approach to better understand the customer's pain points, objections, and core problems implementing your solution. If you jump too quickly to a product-led model with a new category, you risk a high churn rate because you simply don't understand what it takes for customers to succeed.

If you don't have successful customers, a product-led model may amplify the problem. Before you go down the product-led route, make sure you know what goes into customer success.

Cons of a sales-led go-to-market strategy

1. High customer acquisition costs (CAC)

A big downside of the high-touch sales model is that the CAC is out of control, and the sales cycles are extremely long. As you might have guessed, high-touch sales is a leading indicator of CAC.

To make sure the high-touch sales model remains profitable, the LTV of a customer has to be high enough to recoup the investment in acquiring each new customer. To reach that LTV, most sales-led businesses charge their customers a hefty premium. **That premium price isn't because the solution is more valuable but because the customer acquisition model is more expensive.**

As Paul Graham, founder of Y Combinator, states, "The more it costs you to sell something, the more it will cost others to buy it." In short, a sales-led strategy passes costs to consumers that have no connection to product value.

If you currently use a sales-led GTM, you need to watch out for competitors with a more efficient customer acquisition model. They can steal your market share by offering a comparable product with a more affordable price tag.

2. The customer acquisition model is leaky.

In a sales-led organization, the customer acquisition model has a big leak. According to SiriusDecisions, **98% of marketing-qualified leads (MQLs) never result in closed business.**

One reason this conversion rate is famously awful is that the MQL model has a few hidden flaws:

1. It encourages marketers to gate content to hit their MQL goals.

2. It focuses on content consumption as a leading indicator of intent.

3. The entire process rewards creating friction in the buying process.

As a result, there is often a disconnect between marketing and sales. Should we really be surprised? Does downloading a whitepaper mean you're ready to buy? Absolutely not.

3. The organizational structure hinders great product development.

According to Elie Khoury, CEO of Woopra, the typical sales-led business structures their team like the graph below:

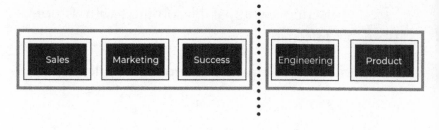

On the left side, you have your profit centre, which handles your sales, marketing, and customer success teams. On the right, you have your cost centre, which creates the product.

The problem with this organizational structure is that the product is often an afterthought. If the sales team closes a really big customer on the condition of a few product tweaks, well, the engineering and product team have a new project to do.

When your organization leads with sales and follows with product, you're forced to move upmarket and get on the elephant-hunting treadmill. And it's not just my opinion.

Case Study

These are the exact words from the CEO of a company[11] that recently raised a Series C from great investors, is growing rapidly, has strong customer retention, and a top-notch leadership team.

My biggest regret is that our first customer was $1M ACV. Ever since that first customer, our product, go-to-market, our support model have all been pulled in one direction—high-end enterprise. Our first $1M ACV customer forced us to get on the elephant hunting treadmill, and we've never been able to get off it. Our board, our employees, everyone expects us to only go after customers that were as large or larger than our first customer. And I've been watching this new competitor emerge that's going after the same market as we are, except from the low end. They are tiny but growing rapidly. And it's too hard for us to compete with them—we don't have the people, technology stack, support model or frankly, the mindset.

His words[12] reinforced something I have long believed: **Truly great SaaS companies are built to be product-led.**

Why SaaS businesses are opting to be product-led

"The future of growth belongs to product-led companies. At HubSpot, we realized this a few years ago, which is why we disrupted our own business model before anyone else could.

At the time, HubSpot was still growing 30%-40% per year on the shoulders of our original marketing and sales driven inbound marketing model. Despite the success, we consciously chose to upend what had been working by launching our first freemium products.

Market dynamics and consumer behavior have changed - increasingly consumers expect to use software and extract value from it **before buying**. To stay relevant over the long term we needed to adapt, or risk "getting our lunch eaten."

– Kieran Flanagan, VP of Marketing, HubSpot

Over the years, countless SaaS businesses have opted to switch from a sales-led GTM to a product-led GTM strategy to create a moat around their business. This is the same strategy that many respected software companies have adopted, including Grammarly, Slack, and Dropbox.

What makes product-led organizations unique is that

they lead with the product across every department, according to Woopra's Khoury.

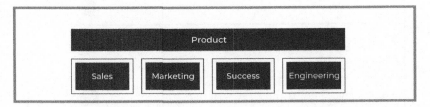

Having the product team involved throughout the business allows for product-led businesses to create a seamless customer experience across every department. What makes a product-led business unique is that all teams leverage the product to hit their goals.

A **product-led marketing** team asks, "How can we use our product as the #1 lead magnet?"

A **product-led sales** team asks, "How can we use the product to qualify our prospects for us? That way, we have conversations with people that already understand our value."

The **product-led customer success** team asks, "How can we create a product that helps customers become successful without our help?"

While the **product-led engineering** team asks, "How can we create a product with a quick time-to-value?"

As you can see in the graph below, a product-led GTM strategy puts you in the safety zone for each tsunami.

Tidal Waves	Safety Zone
Tidal Wave 1 – Self-Educate	☑
Tidal Wave 2 – Rising Acquisition Costs	☑
Tidal Wave 3 – Product Experience	☑

Even though the product-led approach can put your business in a great position to dominate your market, it isn't without its risks. **Implementing a successful Product-Led Growth strategy is difficult.**

This is one of the main reasons I'm writing this book. Product-Led Growth isn't easy to implement. It's not just giving people the option to try your product before they buy. Your entire approach as an organization needs to shift. Instead of leading with sales and following with product, you need to make sure that every team has a hand in helping each user become successful.

If you can put together a successful Product-Led Growth strategy, you'll reap some incredible rewards.

Pros of Product-Led Growth

Product-led businesses have an unfair advantage and enjoy access to a dominant growth engine and significantly lower CACs.

1. Dominant growth engine

Product-led businesses tend to scale faster than their competitors in two powerful ways:

1. **Wider top-of-funnel**. A free trial or freemium model opens up your funnel to people earlier in the customer journey. This is powerful because, instead of prospects filling out your competitor's demo requests, they're evaluating your product.

2. **Rapid global scale.** While your competitors are busy hiring new sales reps for each region under the sun, you can focus on improving your onboarding to service more customers around the world in a fraction of the time.

2. A significantly lower CAC

Free software also builds a moat around your business in three powerful ways:

1. **Faster sales cycles:** By having your prospects onboard themselves, you can significantly reduce your prospect's time-to-value and sales cycle. Once people experience the value in your product, the next logical thing to do is upgrade. The quicker your users can accomplish a key outcome in your product, the quicker you can convert your free users into paying customers.

2. **High revenue-per-employee (RPE):** Software was always built to scale well, but with a prod-

uct-led approach, you're able to do more with fewer people on your team. Less hand-holding means higher profit margins per customer. Just take a look at Ahrefs in 2019. They have a $40 million ARR business with 40 employees.

3. **Better user experience:** Since your product is built for people to onboard themselves, people can experience meaningful value in your product without any hand-holding.

The benefits of a product-led GTM strategy don't stop there. According to OpenView,[13] product-led businesses are valued more than 30% higher than the public-market SaaS Index Fund.

What does this mean for you?

This is not for everyone. You don't *need* to be a product-led business. If you don't know what you're doing, adopting a product-led GTM strategy might kill your business instead of helping it.

Many ambitious entrepreneurs have tried and failed. Rob Walling, the previous CEO of Drip, offers a warning: "Freemium is like a Samurai sword: unless you're a master at using it, you can cut your arm off."

Part of the reason many SaaS businesses fail to transition from a traditional sales-led strategy to a product-led one is that there's no battle-tested playbook. You need to figure out whether a free trial or freemium model will work for your business.

To help make this process easier, I created a decision framework to help you decide whether a free-trial, freemium, or demo model will work best.

CHAPTER 2

Choose Your Weapon—Free Trial, Freemium, or Demo?

When deciding between a free-trial, freemium, or demo model, you need to be extremely careful. Choosing the wrong model can easily bankrupt your business. Unfortunately, you can't just Google the pros and cons or ask a fellow founder which model will work best for you.

Why not? Because that advice comes from people managing *completely* different businesses—different target audiences, different pricing strategies, and different products, which may range from "simple and familiar" to "how on earth do I even use this thing?"

What works for them won't necessarily work for you. To make the right choice, **you need a decision framework** to compare the free-trial, freemium, and demo models.

In this chapter, we'll walk through my **MOAT frame-**

work to help you pick the right go-to-market strategy for your business:

1. **M**arket Strategy: Is your go-to-market strategy dominant, disruptive, or differentiated?

2. **O**cean Conditions: Are you in a red- or blue-ocean business?

3. **A**udience: Do you have a top-down or bottom-up marketing strategy?

4. **T**ime-to-value: How fast can you showcase value?

Let's quickly go over the difference between a free trial and freemium model so we're on the same page.

What's the difference between a free trial or freemium model?

A free trial is a customer acquisition model that provides a partial or complete product to prospects free of charge for a limited time.

A freemium model is a customer acquisition model that provides access to part of a software product to prospects free of charge, without a time limit.

Now, it might seem like freemium is just an indefinite free trial, but the go-to-market strategies could not be more different. Once you know your go-to-market strategy, it will become much easier to decide between a free trial, freemium, or demo model for your business.

Market Strategy: Is your growth strategy dominant, disruptive, or differentiated?

These aren't the *only* go-to-market approaches. In Tony Ulwick's jobs-to-be-done growth matrix,[14] he broke down the five most common growth strategies for any business. However, I'm going to highlight only the differentiated, dominant, and disruptive strategies. They work best if you want to grow quickly.

As you can see in the graph below, these three growth strategies each have a unique advantage:

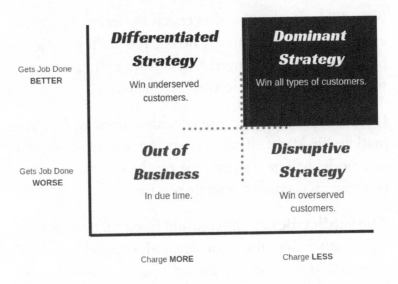

Dominant SaaS Growth Strategy

The dominant growth strategy works great if you can

do something much better than your market *and* can charge significantly less. Companies that employ the dominant growth strategy include:

- Netflix;

- Uber;

- Shopify.

The freemium model is vital in a dominant growth strategy and can help you take a sizable chunk out of a market. How big a market? Well, Jason Lemkin,[15] the founder of SaaStr, argues that you need 50 million active users for freemium to work.

Now, I'd argue that you don't need *that* many. Not every entrepreneur wants to create a $100 million unicorn business, but you do need a significant volume of users for the math to work in your favor.

If you have a niche product with a total addressable market (TAM) of 50 customers, good luck. A freemium model will give away your product to the precious few users who might actually pay for it.

The verdict: Both freemium and free-trial models work much better than the traditional sales model (i.e. demo requests) in the dominant growth strategy because you keep costs low and prevent competitors from stealing your market share. That's your competitive advantage: low cost for an exceptional product.

Questions to ask yourself when deciding if a dominant growth strategy is right for you:

1. Is your TAM big enough to support a freemium model?

2. Does your product solve a specific job significantly better and at a lower cost than anyone else in the market?

3. Can your user realize significant ongoing value quickly with little-to-no help from company personnel?

4. Do you want to be the undisputed market leader in your category?

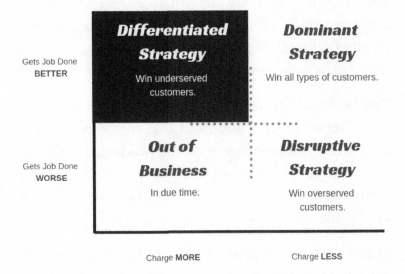

Differentiated SaaS Growth Strategy

This is a common strategy if you want to pick (and win) your fight with an industry goliath.

Your main line of defense against the goliath in your market is specialization. For instance, if you were to take away part of HubSpot's CRM market share, you might discover an underserved niche (e.g. real estate agents) and create a CRM product tailored to that audience.

Differentiated growth requires you to do a specific job better than the competition and charge significantly more. This is not a one-size-fits-all model.

This approach works well with free trials and demos. However, due to the inherent specialization and complexity of these products, it's difficult to create a freemium experience with a quick time-to-value.

Takeaway: Both free trials and demos work great with a differentiated approach, but due to the market-size limitations and complexity of the product, a freemium model often will not work in this environment. Your competitive advantage is how you solve your customer's problems.

Questions to ask yourself when deciding if a differentiated growth strategy is right for you:

1. Is your market comprised of underserved customers?

2. What is your TAM?

3. Is your Annual Contract Value (ACV) high enough to support a low- or high-touch sales team?

4. Could your prospects experience an "Aha!" moment during a free trial?

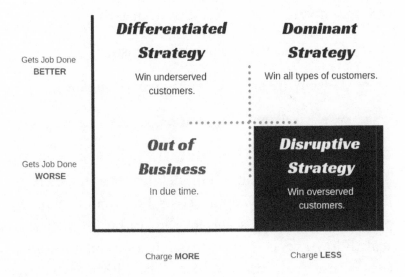

Disruptive SaaS Growth Strategy

Most fast-growing SaaS companies are labelled "disruptors," but don't let the label fool you. Few ever deploy a disruptive growth strategy.

Why? The disruptive growth approach requires you to charge less for what many might consider an "inferior product." Most people think this is a bad idea, but it's not. If you've used Canva (a simple custom-graphic tool), you've witnessed this first hand. If you compare Adobe Photoshop's features against those of Canva, Canva loses every time—by a lot.

But with so many over-served customers in this particular market, Canva was able to build a much simpler product that solved very specific pain points, such as creating social media graphics in seconds. Quite a few other companies have taken this approach:

- Google Docs (relative to Microsoft Word);

- Udacity (relative to traditional universities);

- Wave (relative to traditional accounting software).

Takeaway: The freemium model thrives in the disruptive environment. Keeping costs low draws in prospects using existing solutions. Since the product is a scaled-down version of an existing solution, it must be easy to use. You can use a free trial with a disruptive growth strategy, but it weakens the "magnetic draw" enjoyed by the freemium model.

Questions to ask yourself when deciding if a disruptive growth strategy is right for you:

1. Is your market full of over-served customers?

2. Are you competing in a hyper-competitive market?

3. Is your market large enough to support a freemi-

um model? (Hint: Look to your competitors to gauge the market size.)

4. Do you have the resources to support a freemium model?

5. Can your onboarding be completely self-service?

Activity: Make a decision on your growth strategy

By now, I want you to decide whether your SaaS product follows a dominant, differentiated, or disruptive growth strategy.

Questions to ask yourself when deciding on your market strategy:

1. Do you want to offer the best solution for the lowest price? (Dominant strategy)

2. Do you want to offer the best-customized solution for the highest price to underserved customers? (Differentiated strategy)

3. Do you want to offer the simplest product for the lowest price to over-served customers? (Disruptive strategy)

4. Or are you planning on using a hybrid strategy?

Once you know your market strategy, you need to validate that it's suited to external factors in your market. One of the best ways to vet your market strategy is by understanding whether you're in a red- or blue-ocean business.

CHAPTER 3

Ocean Conditions: Are You in a Red- or Blue-Ocean Business?

Before we dive into how your ocean strategy will affect your Product-Led Growth model, I want to explain the difference between blue- and red-ocean companies.[16]

Red-ocean companies try to outperform their rivals to grab a greater share of existing demand. As the market gets crowded, prospects for profits and growth reduce. Products become commodities, and cut-throat competition turns the bloody ocean red.

Blue-ocean companies access untapped market space and create demand, and so they have the opportunity for highly profitable growth. In Blue Oceans, competition is irrelevant. Yes, imitators arise, but experience shows there is a wide window of opportunity to stay ahead of imitators.

Here's a high-level overview of the differences between the two ocean strategies:

Red-Ocean Strategy (Harvest Demand)	Blue-Ocean Strategy (Create Demand)
Compete in existing markets.	Create uncontested market spaces.
Beat the competition.	Make the competition irrelevant.
Exploit existing demand.	Create and capture new demand.

If you're competing in a red ocean, you're fighting to exploit existing demand, whereas, in a blue ocean, you're creating demand. To determine if you're in a blue or red ocean, you can't simply ask, "Am I creating or harvesting demand?" It's also not enough to look at your market, label the competitors, and assume that you're in a bloody red ocean.

Within your market, some segments could be in a red ocean while others are in blue oceans. For instance, one of my clients in the business intelligence (BI) software space knew the enterprise side of the BI market was a bloody red ocean. So, they strategically focused on small and medium-sized businesses where they could operate in a blue ocean—same market, different ocean strategy.

Now, drill down into the market segment that you're targeting. It might not be as competitive as you think.

When It Comes to Product-led Growth, Why Does This Matter?

Growing a business in a blue or red ocean requires a different approach. Here's what matters:

Blue Ocean

If you're in a blue ocean and creating demand, your product may have a steep learning curve. Before you can make the sale, you need to educate your market on why your new way of doing something is better.

Take Salesforce. When they first launched, the sales team had to educate potential customers on why a cloud-based CRM made sense. The sales team met resistance from companies that, among other objections, worried about their data being lost or stolen.

Had Salesforce started with a no-touch, product-led model, it would have been hard, if not impossible, to combat those objections. As a result, most people wouldn't buy the product. You don't become a market behemoth by selling products nobody can understand. For this reason, most companies leverage a sales or marketing-driven go-to-market strategy in a blue ocean.

That said, if you have a simple application like Spotify that can help users experience the value of your product almost immediately, you can still lead with a Product-Led Growth model.

Takeaway: If you're in a blue ocean and have a quick time-to-value in your product, use a product-led model. However, if your product is complex, start with a sales-led go-to-market strategy to educate your audience and create demand. Still, ask "when" not "if" you're going to launch a product-led arm of the business.

Red Ocean

In a red ocean, prospects already know how your product can help them, and a product-led model is advantageous—it can widen your funnel, decrease your CAC, and help you expand globally in a fraction of the time.

A Product-Led Growth model also helps you convert "non-customers"—people who typically won't reach out to request pricing or sign up for a demo request. However, these non-customers are willing to try your product and, if it's right for them, buy it.

This trend—though not a rule—is shared among the hundreds of SaaS businesses I've analyzed:

- Blue Ocean businesses lead with a sales-led GTM.

- Red Ocean businesses lead with a product-led GTM.

Take live-chat software as an example. When it first came to market, most companies started with traditional sales-led GTM strategies. Once the category matured, it became almost impossible to find a live-chat application without a product-led model. As Pankaj Prasad, Director of Product Management at Salesforce, argues, "Product-led is the only distribution model worth undertaking once the market is mature."

Takeaway: If you're in a red ocean, use a product-led model to widen your funnel, decrease your CAC, and expand globally. You need to grow as fast and profitably as possible.

Questions to ask yourself when deciding between a blue or red ocean:

1. Am I creating or capturing existing demand?

2. Does the product have a quick time-to-value?

3. Will a marketing, sales, or product-led GTM suit my business the best?

Before deciding if Product-Led Growth is right for you, make sure you're targeting the right audience.

CHAPTER 4

Audience: Do You Have a Top-Down or Bottom-Up Selling Strategy?

Traditionally, it made sense to sell SaaS products only to executives at the top. After all, these decision-makers had to sign off on major purchases.

Nowadays, the tables have turned. Products are a fraction of the price they used to be, and, in many cases, you don't need to talk to a sales rep to purchase a product. Instead of executives making all the purchasing decisions, front-line employees hold the same power.

Slack is a perfect example of a bottom-up selling strategy. The product spreads organically, typically starting with one user who invites a colleague—then an entire team—to join. Product use reaches a tipping point at which the team manager invests in Slack because it has become invaluable. This strategy of leading with value took Slack from zero to a $4 billion valuation in three years.

Now, whether you employ a top-down or bottom-up selling strategy, you need to know which strategy works best for your business. Let's dive into the differences between the two selling strategies.

What is a top-down selling strategy?

Companies that use the top-down selling strategy: SAP, Oracle, and IBM.

When using a top-down selling strategy, your sales team targets key decision-makers and executives. Typically, these deals include large product rollouts throughout an entire business.

One reason the top-down sales strategy exists is that businesses want uniformity. Decision makers like to keep their businesses organized and allocate resources efficiently. It doesn't make sense to use a different CRM for each local sales team when you can use one for everyone.

If you're selling large deals, top-down systems are essential. Typically, the larger the sale, the more service and training a customer requires. Take SAP. When sold, new customers need additional training and resources to put the product to good use. It's not unheard of for enterprise software purchases to take 12–16 months for the internal team to understand how to get value from the software.

With a top-down selling strategy, you'll typically make the sale to the decision-makers at the top of the organization. But the real selling has just begun. Now, you have to convince internal teams to use your software.

What is a bottom-up selling strategy?

Companies that use the bottom-up selling strategy: Slack, DocuSign, and Atlassian.

Bottom-up selling strategies are the norm in the consumer market. Take Facebook, Twitter, or Evernote: Each created a product that can be adopted in minutes. Unlike the top-down selling strategy, where it may take months or years to close a sale (and another year to understand how to use the product), bottom-up selling strategies demand quick adoption and simplicity.

Typically, businesses deploy a free-trial or freemium model to make a bottom-up selling strategy work. A big reason to choose a product-led model is that if people can't see the value in using your product quickly, few will upgrade.

Before you decide on a top-down or bottom-up selling strategy, let's quickly go through some of the benefits of each strategy.

What are the pros and cons of top-down and bottom-up selling strategies?

When deciding between a top-down and bottom-up selling strategy, consider your go-to-market strategy:

- A top-down selling strategy pairs well with a sales-led go-to-market strategy.

- A bottom-up selling strategy works almost exclusively with a product-led go-to-market strategy.

As we go through each selling strategy, pay attention to which model resembles your business.

Benefits of a Top-Down Selling Strategy

1. **High ACV.** Employing a top-down selling strategy almost always results in more significant contracts. If you're starting out, this can be a great way to boost your monthly recurring revenue fast.

2. **Additional Services.** Top-down selling strategies often benefit from selling additional training and services. Selling these services isn't a guarantee but is often needed with large product rollouts.

3. **Low Customer Churn.** Given that implementing product rollouts is expensive and time-consuming, most customers are reluctant to change products. As long as your product solves the

customer's pain points adequately, you can usually count on these customers to continue paying for your product.

If you're selling to the enterprise, you often deal with a significantly lower churn rate than other market segments, according to Brianne Kimmel:[17]

Segment	Monthly Customer Churn %	Annual Customer Churn %
SMB	3–7%	31–58%
Mid-Market	1–2%	11–22%
Enterprise	0.5–1%	6–10%

Like anything, a top-down selling strategy has significant downsides.

Disadvantages of a Top-Down Selling Strategy

1. **Poor revenue distribution.** Relationships are the growth engine of top-down selling. Often, your sales team will target "whales." Although I think it's rude to refer to buyers as whales, it's what a lot of sales teams use to refer to big buyers. When it comes to top-down selling, you have to be okay with a large percentage of total revenue coming from one place. Losing one contract can result in a sharp (and often unpredicted) decline in revenue.

2. **High CAC.** Given the sheer number of hours it takes to build relationships with key decision-makers, your CAC will be substantial with a top-down selling strategy. It should come as no surprise that high-touch sales are a leading indicator of CAC.

3. **Long Sales Cycles.** In addition to a high CAC, the sales cycle typically takes a long time to finalize.

Remember: Once the contract is signed, the sale has just begun. Afterward, you need to convince people at the bottom to use the application. While this is not necessarily a disadvantage, some middle management will work against the product rollout if they didn't want it in the first place.

To recap, here is a high-level overview of a top-down selling strategy:

Benefits	Disadvantages
Lower churn	Long sales cycle
Selling additional service	High CAC
Large sale value	Bad revenue distribution

Now, let's dive into why you might want to consider a bottom-up selling strategy.

Benefits of a Bottom-Up Selling Strategy

Your product is your growth engine for a bottom-up selling strategy. Your product is responsible for onboarding users, showcasing its value, and even upgrading users. In many organizations with a bottom-up selling strategy, you don't even need to talk to someone for them to buy your product. Netflix and Spotify are perfect examples.

In the B2B space, most products employ a low-touch, bottom-up sales model in which sales reps target users who take specific actions in the product. These are the top six benefits of a bottom-up selling strategy:

1. **Wider top-of-funnel.** A free-trial or freemium model opens the funnel to people earlier in their customer journey.

2. **Lower CAC.** Since there's minimal interaction with the sales team, the CAC is often significantly lower with a bottom-up selling strategy. Another benefit of the bottom-up selling strategy is that middle management is often rooting for you to win because they're the ones championing your product to the company.

3. **Predictable sales figures.** With a bottom-up selling strategy, you can see how many free-trial and freemium users are in your funnel and what percentage of them will upgrade at any given time. Compare this to the top-down selling

strategy, where it's almost impossible to predict when a deal will close.

4. **Revenue diversity.** The bottom-up selling strategy often has a much smaller deal size. You can attract a broader market and profitably service more customers than competitors with a top-down selling strategy. Doing so spreads your revenue among many customers, and losing one customer doesn't cause a painful blow to your revenue.

5. **Scale globally fast.** While competitors are busy setting up expensive offices throughout the world, you can hone your onboarding to help more users across the globe succeed quickly and cheaply.

Case Study

Andrew Bieda of Landingi, for example, is a master at a rapid global scale with a free trial and paid acquisition channels like Facebook and Google. Andrew's team looks for markets with optimal CPC, sign-up acquisition costs, and trial-to-paid conversion rates, allowing them to pursue new markets where he can profitably acquire new customers and avoid ones that are oversaturated with competition.

6. **Fast sales cycles.** By having users onboard themselves, you can significantly reduce your prospect's time-to-value and sales cycle.

All in all, a bottom-up selling strategy has some incredible advantages to help you scale your business faster, but it's not without its challenges.

Disadvantages of a Bottom-Up Selling Strategy

The main disadvantages are financial.

1. **Contract size.** For one, the contract size is often significantly smaller than the top-down selling strategy. You need a higher number of sales to make ends meet. As we mentioned in the benefits section, this can also be a blessing in disguise—losing one customer won't cripple your business.

2. **Non-paying customers.** If you launch a freemium product and don't know what you're doing, you could easily wind up with a significant portion of non-paying customers. This often happens when a product gives away too much for free, and users have no reason to upgrade—the free plan suits their everyday needs. Luckily, you can fix this problem, but it's tough to get someone to pay for something they've been using for free.

3. **Significant investment.** Non-paying customers are a drain on resources. Customer support can become overwhelmed, and sales wastes time on users who are satisfied with the free product, among other resource drains.

4. **Expertise shortage.** Finding someone exceptional at launching and optimizing a free-trial or freemium product is exceedingly rare. These people are in demand because so many businesses are trying to adopt a bottom-up selling strategy.

If you have the resources, hire a Product-Led Growth expert or consultant to help launch and optimize your free trial or freemium model. It may be expensive upfront, but they can save you hundreds of hours and millions in sales. If you don't have the resources, expect to spend lots of time experimenting and trying to figure out what works.

To recap, here's a high-level overview of the benefits and disadvantages of a bottom-up selling strategy:

Bottom-Up Benefits	Bottom-Up Disadvantages
Low touch	Smaller contract size
Lower CAC	Significant investment
Faster sales cycles	Non-paying customers
Predictability in sales figures	Expertise drain

What selling strategy is right for you?

As a kid, one of my favorite pastimes was trying to make the positive ends of two magnets touch each other. If you've done this before, you know that the magnets repel each other.

I bring up this story because your selling strategy has to align with your go-to-market strategy. If your product has a freemium model and a top-down selling strategy, the two approaches will repel each other. However, if you align your product-led model with your selling strategy, you'll have unmatchable synergy.

That strategic alignment (unlike magnets) is not science, but here's how Product-Led Growth models fit with selling strategies:

Product-Led Growth Model	Selling Strategy	Outcome
Freemium	Top-Down	Unsuccessful
Freemium	Bottom-Up	Successful
Free Trial	Top-Down	Mixed Results
Free Trial	Bottom-Up	Successful

Freemium and top-down selling. The freemium model rarely works with a top-down selling strategy for a few reasons. First, you're expecting decision-makers and executives to understand how to use your product.

Most decision-makers won't be everyday users of the product, so it doesn't make sense to onboard them in the first place.

Freemium or free trial and bottom-up selling. If you go with a bottom-up selling strategy that attracts middle management and teams, you help your potential buyers use the product, experience meaningful value, and make the case to purchase your solution to upper management.

Free trial and top-down selling. Having a free trial with a top-down selling strategy is a grey area. When I was working at a B2B SaaS startup, we employed a top-down selling strategy and a free trial. But after people signed up, there was no onboarding, no helpful emails, and no support. The experience was bad.

When we suggested changes to the engineering team, we were shut down. The Chief Technology Officer wanted to treat the free trial as a pseudo demo request. This scenario might sound unusual, but it's widespread. If a company employs a top-down selling strategy, they have the systems and expertise in place to convert demo requests into customers. Teams have demo request goals, and a free trial cannibalizes demo requests.

In this example, it didn't take long until the company removed the free-trial option from the website. It was a shame. It could have worked, but everyone was so focused on hitting their short-term revenue targets for the quarter that the free trial just got in the way.

If you've caught yourself in this situation—where management directly opposes supporting and improving the free-trial experience—it's generally a fool's errand to try to fix the situation unless you're an executive or can show some incredible (and rapid) results. To be successful, you need executive buy-in and realistic expectations when the free trial launches.

To recap, top-down selling puts the burden on the sales team. A bottom-up approach lets the prospective customer discover the product's value on their own.

Questions to ask yourself when deciding between a top-down or bottom-up selling approach:

- Are you currently targeting people who can easily use your product and experience its value?

- What is your ACV for each customer? Is it high enough to justify a low- or high-touch sales model?

Unfortunately, none of this matters unless you can showcase the value of your product, fast.

CHAPTER 5

Time-to-Value: How Fast Can You Showcase Value?

"From a marketing and sales perspective, Product-Led Growth is a game-changer. It means you can deliver on your promise to prospects. It also means the product sells itself if you get in front of people at the right stage of the buying process."

- Juliana Casale, Head of Marketing, CrazyEgg

To create a successful product-led business, you need a quick time-to-value. New users need to be able to experience a key outcome in your product quickly and without any assistance. If your users require extensive hand-holding to get a glimpse of value, most will never return after signing up.

This isn't just my opinion. Intercom claims that 40–

60% of new users never come back after signing up. To help pinpoint your product's time-to-value, analyze your existing user base. Regardless of your product or industry, these are the four types of users:

- **Mission Impossible Users.** Your user has low motivation and finds it hard, if not impossible, to use your product.

- **Rookie Users.** Your user has high motivation but finds it incredibly difficult to use your product. This scenario is often a luxury for companies. It usually pops up when employees are forced to use existing software or have no alternative solutions.

- **Veteran Users.** Your user has low motivation but finds it easy to use your product. This means your user will accomplish the target behavior easily but could flee at any sign of friction—or hunger. Who knows?!

- **Spoiled Users.** This is the outcome to optimize for. Your user has high motivation and finds it straightforward to use your product. This means that you'll help the greatest number of people in your Total Addressable Market (TAM).

In the graph below, I challenge you to identify the top two user types who sign up for your product.

Now, **which users are you most familiar with?** If all you have is spoiled users, bravo. If not, you need to work on improving your time-to-value. The good news is that there are so many things that you can do to improve it:

- Want to strengthen user motivation? Hire a great copywriter.

- Want to increase the number of people who complete account setup? Eliminate unnecessary steps in your onboarding.

In contrast to the ocean you compete in, you have control over your time-to-value. In Part III, I'll dive deep to show you how you can improve it. In the meantime, ask yourself these questions to narrow down whether a free-trial, freemium, or demo model will work best for you:

- How motivated are users when they sign up for your product?

- Is your product easy for your target audience to use?

- Can users experience the core value of your product without hand-holding?

CHAPTER 6

Choose Your Product-Led Growth Model with the MOAT Framework

B y now, you should have a much better idea as to whether a sales- or Product-Led Growth model will work best for your business. If you're confident that Product-Led Growth is right, you need to decide between a free trial or freemium model.

Having helped hundreds of business owners make this difficult decision, I created a simple quiz to help you pinpoint which model is best for you. Go to productled.com/quiz and answer a series of questions to see which makes sense for your business. Share it with your team and see if they get similar results.

One thing to note is that you can answer these same questions at a different stage in your business and get completely different results. I've built the quiz to adapt as your business and market matures.

Regardless of whether the quiz tells you to use a free trial or freemium model, consider whether a hybrid model might work, too. Below I outline three of the most common hybrid models.

Hybrid Model 1: Launch a new product

When you're an established business and want to de-risk your business, launching a new product-led arm is a solid option. This allows you to experiment with a product-led model, build the in-house expertise, and vet if the model will work—without disrupting your cash-cow products.

It's an effective strategy. At Vidyard, we tested this strategy by launching GoVideo and refining our freemium go-to-market strategy. It was far from perfect when we launched, but we were able to improve it—and acquire 100,000s of new users in the process. This, in turn, helped the business justify the creation of a small in-house team to bring a freemium product to market.

Hybrid Model 2: Go freemium, with a trial

If you have a product with lots of features, this strategy can work well. As long as your freemium version is valuable, you can layer on free-trial upgrades within the freemium product.

HubSpot has been doing this successfully for a while now. When you sign up for the free marketing and sales tools, you get immediate value from the product. But, as you get more value from the free product, they tempt you with free-trial landing pages for blocked features.

This allows the user to experience the new feature for a limited amount of time before upgrading. For Hub-Spot's sales team, it's also convenient: It acts as a "hand raiser" to cue them to reach out and ensure the user succeeds with the new feature.

Hybrid Model #3: Go free trial, follow with freemium

If you don't convert at the end of Nudge.ai's 30-day free trial, you're prompted to use their free tool. This freemium product sits in Gmail and gives you useful information on each contact in your inbox. In addition to providing value, it's an inexpensive form of advertising and keeps their solution top-of-mind.

There are other ways you can slice and dice hybrid models, too, but these three are the most common. Now, before you dive into Part II, I encourage you to take a break and think about what product-led model will work best for your business. If you're still undecided, I'd recommend taking the product-led quiz at productled.com/quiz to understand which model will work best for your business.. Next up, we're going to dive into how you can build your foundation for a product-led business.

Build Your Foundation

CHAPTER 7

Build a Product-Led Foundation

> Risk comes from not knowing what you're doing.
>
> **- Warren Buffett**

Like any big business decision, building a product-led business can be risky. There are a lot of unknowns along the way. Your free product may cannibalize demo requests. Free users can overwhelm your support team. There's no shortage of potential surprises!

Before I wrote this book, there was only a tiny amount of high-quality information online that showed you how to build a product-led business. And yet, bold entrepreneurs, as they always do, blazed a path ahead anyway. They built product-led businesses before anyone even knew what product-led meant. Uncharted territories is where they thrive!

These founders have created incredible businesses like Atlassian, HubSpot, and Slack. But Product-Led Growth is no longer reserved for the entrepreneur who's willing to risk it all. Not at all.

Product-Led Growth is a life raft that will save you from the flood of rising customer acquisition costs and decreasing willingness to pay for your product. To make Product-Led Growth more accessible, I created this playbook to arm you with the core elements of what it takes to build a successful product-led business. That way, it's less risky.

Whether you're considering launching a product-led model or you want to build a stronger product-led business, you're about to learn what it really takes to make it happen. In this section, we'll go through the UCD framework, which shows you how to build a solid foundation for your product-led business.

As you can see in the graph below, each step builds on the other:

1. **Understand** your value.

2. **Communicate** the perceived value of your product.

3. **Deliver** on what you promise.

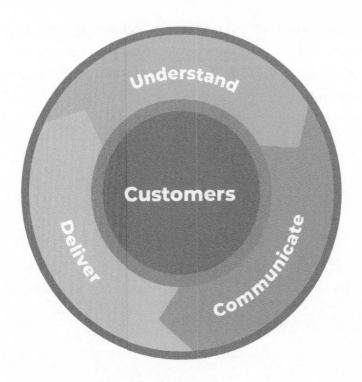

The real value of the UCD framework is that you can apply it to any of these scenarios:

1. You're just launching a business and want to go down the product-led path.

2. You're starting a product-led arm of an existing company.

3. You're transitioning from a sales-led to a product-led business.

4. You want to relaunch your product-led model because it's currently underperforming.

If you skip one step, you risk delivering a mediocre experience to your users. So, please don't skip any. It's not worth it. Let's kick things off with understanding your value.

------ CHAPTER 8 ------

Understand Your Value

Let's say you're selling live-chat software like Intercom. You're not *really* selling live-chat software (fun fact). You're selling a new and better way to acquire customers.

Often, it's easy to think that we sell products based on the functional outcome they accomplish. Businesses need live-chat software, right? No. Businesses do not need live-chat software. But, businesses *do* need a new and better way to acquire customers.

The difference is that we're **selling an outcome.** Businesses will always need to acquire customers. If businesses aren't able to acquire customers, they experience pain—pain that they didn't hit their marketing goals; pain that they can't meet payroll; pain that, well, sucks.

This kind of pain is product agnostic. But pain is also beautiful in a weird way. Pain makes us want to change so that we can avoid it or prevent it altogether. As we go through this chapter, I challenge you to ask yourself: **What outcome do people expect when they buy your product?**

Most technology companies get caught up in the features and don't *really* know why people buy their product. So, they create bland headlines that read, "We sell live-chat software for website and mobile support." From the copy, we know what this business sells, but why choose one option over another? The copy assumes we know the outcome that live chat solves for.

It also shows us that the company didn't take the time to do customer development. As Steve Blank would say, "Cheating on customer development is like cheating on your parachute-packing class." It's not worth it.

To build a successful product-led business, you need to understand the three main outcomes that motivate the purchase of your product. Let's walk through each.

The three reasons that people buy a product

1. Functional Outcome: the core tasks that customers want to get done.

Most businesses can pinpoint what their product does. For instance, people use Google Ads to acquire leads that (hopefully) will turn into customers. For a business intelligence tool, this could be understanding the core KPIs of your business.

Although people take the functional outcome into consideration when buying a product, most companies forget to consider the emotional and social outcomes. If you don't know the emotional or social outcomes people are looking for when buying your product, you could be missing out on some serious profitability.

(This is the difference between someone dishing out $30 for a hamburger at a fancy restaurant versus spending $2.50 on a McDonald's cheeseburger.)

2. Emotional Outcome: how customers want to feel or avoid feeling as a result of executing the core functional outcome.

Understanding your emotional outcome can be tricky. For instance, do you want someone who uses Google Ads to feel empowered to grow their business? Of course! But, do you know if they actually feel empowered? You'll never know until you start asking your customers.

For a business intelligence tool, this could be the feeling of excitement or surprise as you discover a big opportunity (or threat) for your business with new data.

Lastly, you need to understand your social outcome.

3. Social Outcome: how customers want to be perceived by others by using your product.

For Google Ads, this could be showcasing a report of your campaign's performance to your boss. For a business intelligence tool, this could be sharing a weekly revenue report to your executive team that makes you look like a professional designer. Co-workers ask how you put together such an incredible presentation.

If you can understand the three main outcomes behind why people buy your product—and execute on it—you're on the right track to building a strong product-led foundation. The challenge, however, is always in the execution. For instance, if your product offers video hosting but people sign up thinking that you're a video marketing agency, they're doomed from the start. No wizard or product tour can save that. Period.

If you don't know how to do customer research, just sign up at doubleyourtrials.com. It's a free customer research course that has helped thousands identify the three main outcomes behind why people buy their product.

That said, it can be just as valuable to put on your analytics hat and go digging. In every software product, there are usage patterns that point us toward the core outcomes that are most important to our customers. One of the biggest differences between sales- and product-led companies is that the latter consistently monitor these usage patterns to see if users are accomplishing meaningful outcomes.

Because of how valuable monitoring these usage patterns has become to product-led businesses, they're often referred to as "value metrics."

What the Heck Are Value Metrics?

A value metric is the way you measure value exchange in your product.

> "If you're selling a pair of shoes, then your value metric is 'per pair of shoes' and as customers buy more pairs your business expands."
>
> **- ProfitWell**

Ultimately, value metrics are the linchpin to successful execution of a product-led go-to-market strategy. Why? Because you're aligning your revenue model directly with your customer acquisition model.

Your value metrics play a vital role in how you price your product, set up your product metrics, and build your team. But, what the heck does it look like?

- For a video platform like Wistia, a value metric could be the number of videos uploaded.

- For a communication application like Slack, a value metric could be the number of messages sent.

- For a payment processing platform like PayPal, a value metric could be the amount of revenue generated.

According to Patrick Campbell,[18] CEO of ProfitWell, there are two types of value metrics: functional and outcome based. Functional value metrics are "per user" or "per 100 videos." Pricing scales around a function of usage. Outcome-based value metrics charge based on an outcome, like how many views a video received or how much money you made your customer.

Now, many SaaS businesses rely on feature differentiation as a way of justifying higher price points. But this comes at the cost of higher churn. As Campbell notes, value metrics outperform feature differentiation with up to 75% less churn. Outcome-based value metrics take this a step further with an additional 40% reduction in churn.

Campbell continues:

> This trend continues further when looking at expansion revenue. Both types of value metrics still outperform feature differentiated pricing models with at least 30% more expansion revenue, but outcome-based value metrics push those gains to nearly 50%.

> We all don't have the luxury of pricing based on outcome though, because sometimes it's hard to perfectly measure how much money someone gained from using your product or how much that time you saved them is worth. Yet, we can still take a lesson from this data in making sure we get as close to that customer and as close to value as technically possible.

Before we dive into how to find your value metric, let's step back and identify what makes a good value metric.

What Makes a Good Value Metric?

According to Campbell, a great value metric must pass three tests.

1. It's easy for the customer to understand.

When someone visits your pricing page, will they immediately understand what they're paying for and where they fit in your packaging? If not, you need to pick a new value metric.

If you're in an established market, it makes sense to view how your competitors charge. A common value metric might be used by most competitors. For instance, if you're in the email marketing space, most solutions charge by the number of contacts you have, so it makes sense to use contacts as your value metric.

However, if you're in an emerging space like artificial intelligence, you'll want to opt for a more data-driven approach to discover your value metric, something we'll cover later in this chapter.

In addition to making it easy for your customers to understand your value metric, make sure that your value metric aligns with the value that customers receive by using the product.

2. It's aligned with the value that the customer receives in the product.

Consider the low-level components of your high-level outcome. If that sounds confusing, let me reframe it. Let's say you have a live-chat solution. If you want to acquire more customers, you need to monitor how many messages customers have on their website with your live-chat solution. By monitoring the number of conversations, you're able to see, at a high level, how much value they're getting.

Or, if you run a churn-prevention solution, you need to monitor how many customers set up automated emails that prevent churn due to credit card failures. Depending on how many emails are sent to recover churned customers, you can easily see your impact on saved revenue.

In both examples, we're simply looking for what it takes to achieve a specific outcome. When it comes to your product, **what core components lead someone to experience a meaningful outcome?**

- Is it the number of contacts used by your CRM?

- Is it the number of live-chat conversations started?

You tell me!

Lastly, make sure that your value metric grows with your customer.

3. Grows with your customer's usage of that value.

If customers get incredible value from your product, charge them more—your product is worth it. On the flip side, if customers aren't getting the full value from your product, charge them less.

Slack does a great job emphasizing this on their pricing page by creating a fair billing policy. Given that Slack's value metric is the number of users you add to the messaging platform, it makes sense to charge per user.

However, if you're an enterprise with a large number of users, one of your biggest objections is not knowing how many people are actually going to use the platform. To combat this, Slack created the fair billing policy—you get charged only for active users.

Although it's easy to suggest what makes a good value metric, it's even easier to choose the wrong one.

The Mistake that So Many Make: User-Based Pricing

One of the most common traps is charging per user. For many businesses, charging per user is like tying a rope to an anchor that's already tied to your feet, then tossing the anchor overboard. You're going to get dragged down until you figure out how to cut the rope and pick a new value metric.

As ProfitWell's Patrick Campbell explains, "The reason per user pricing kills your growth and sets you up for long term failure is because it's rarely where the value is ascribed to your product."

If you get charged by the user, are you going to share that product throughout your entire team? Or are you going to limit the usage to a select few? If you have a messaging application like Slack, it's perfectly fine to charge by the user—the product has network effects and gets more valuable with more people.

But Slack is the exception, not the rule. So why is user pricing still the most common way people price solutions, according to the Pacific Crest Survey?[19] Part of the reason is that companies just don't know better. Most companies don't have anyone to evaluate objectively if per-user pricing makes sense. Why?

"It's counterintuitive," Campbell notes,[20] "but because pricing touches on every single part of your business, it's often ignored. That's because it's at the intersection of marketing, sales, and product—so nobody in the organization owns it."

If you think about it, this happens all the time in volleyball. Whenever the ball goes directly between four players, everyone assumes someone else will get the ball, so nobody actually gets it. Don't you hate when that happens?

Openview created a checklist to help identify whether user-based pricing makes sense for your business. If you can check "True" for each of these conditions, per-user pricing is a great fit. If not, well, at least you know that it's not the right fit. Better now than never, right?

Per-User Pricing Scratch Pad

Condition	Example	True?
Each user receives differentiated value from accessing the product.	LinkedIn Recruiter	
The customer has a strong need to standardize their department or company on the platform.	Salesforce	
The product has network effects, where initial users want to collaborate and invite others.	Slack	
Budget predictability and control is critical for your buyer persona(s).	DocuSign	
Buyer is less sophisticated and needs easy-to-understand pricing.	Evernote	
Usage metrics in your industry have become commoditized or are becoming table stakes.	GitHub	

Now that we've covered what makes a good and bad value metric, it's time to define yours. This is the fun part!

How to find your value metric

Finding your value metrics helps you monitor if users are achieving meaningful outcomes in your product. They also play a critical role in reshaping your pricing strategy.

Choosing your value metric doesn't need to be complicated—you don't even need to get it right the very first time. If you're a small company, you can afford to test several hypotheses (as long as you take a data-driven approach).

I'll go through two different strategies that—depending on your company size—can help define your value metric. For best results, I'd recommend using both approaches in unison.

Step 1: Subjective Analysis

By now, you should have at least a couple of hypotheses about your value metric:

- Is it messages sent?

- Number of users?

- Total revenue generated?

Pull out a piece of paper and jot down everything you think could be a value metric. Once you have the list, run it through the value metric scratch pad.

Value Metric Scratch Pad

Condition	True?
It's easy for the customer to understand.	
It's aligned with the value that the customer receives in the product..	
It grows with your customer's usage of that value.	

How did your value metrics stack up? Did you find a value metric that works? If not, stop reading this book and continue to brainstorm new value metrics until you have one that passes these three conditions. I can wait.

Everything from this point on focuses on how to help your users experience this value metric in your product as quickly and often as possible. It can be tempting to call it quits once you've found a value metric that you think will work, but, given the importance of the metric, I encourage you to vet your metric with a data-driven approach.

Step 2: Data-Driven Approach

Every SaaS business has many types of users. You'll have users who churn quickly, users who barely use your product, power users, and users with an extremely high lifetime value.

When analyzing usage patterns, it's easy to focus on

measuring your product data without segmenting your users. By doing so, it's easy to optimize for everyone while creating a worse experience for your best users.

For instance, if we look at the product data for your best customers, we could streamline the onboarding experience for your perfect-fit customers while simultaneously filtering out bad-fit customers. We might decrease our signup-to-activation metric but increase our free-to-paid conversion rate.

To get meaningful insights out of your product data, look for patterns among your best and worst customers. For instance, ask yourself these questions when analyzing your data:

1. What do my best customers do regularly in the product?

2. What do my best customers not do in the product?

3. What features did my best users try first during onboarding?

4. What similarities among my best users—demographics, team structure, ability—led to success?

For churned customers, ask:

1. What were some of the main differences between their user journey and that of your best customer?

2. Specifically, what activities were different? What outcomes did your churned users achieve and not achieve?

3. Were these churned customers in your target market?

4. Why did the majority of these customers churn?

When trying to answer these questions, go through your product data to validate everything. And I really do mean everything. After you've come up with several viable value metrics, stress test their potential.

How to Stress Test Your Value Metrics

Using a value metric scratch pad is one of the easiest ways to validate if you have the right value metric.

Value Metric Scratch Pad

Condition	True?
It's easy for the customer to understand.	
It's aligned with the value that the customer receives in the product.	
It grows with your customer's usage of that value.	

However, there's a downsides: A simple scratch pad is based on your insights, not your customers'. To take it a step further, use a relative preference analysis. This is a simple statistical method to measure value in your product. You force people to make a decision between what they most and least want.

Here's an example of what it could look like from ProfitWell:

In terms of [company] pricing, which of the following when it comes to pricing is most preferred? Least preferred?

Value Metric	Most Preferred	Least Prefered
Analytics	X	
Premium Support		
Integrations		
SLA		
Single Sign-On		X

Once you've asked enough people, you can identify the ideal value metric. Now, it's time to communicate your value metric to your audience.

CHAPTER 9

Communicate Your Value

Communicating your value is at the crux of a Product-Led Growth strategy. Sales-led companies love to hide their pricing behind closed doors, asking potential buyers to request the price. Product-led companies eliminate this unnecessary friction with up-front pricing for most starter plans.

As a result, one of the most common "side projects" when launching a free trial or freemium model is re-hauling the pricing page. Why?

For companies transitioning from a sales-led to product-led business, most previously hid their pricing. Others required businesses to pay for specific features that are now given away for free as an incentive to encourage signups for free accounts.

Communicating your value warrants an entire chapter because, in a product-led business, **your revenue and customer acquisition model are married together.**

(It's an arranged marriage, but a marriage nonetheless.) In a sales-led business, the revenue and customer acquisition models are separated.

A sales-led business can bank on relationships to sell large contracts. In a product-led company, your customer acquisition model is built around your product. If your product sucks, you're not making payroll this month. If your revenue model is confusing, the number of people signing up for your free trial or freemium model will take a hit. This is why you need to dial in your acquisition and revenue models.

If not, you're headed for an early divorce. As your product-led preacher, I just can't let that happen—it's heresy. Here's how to prevent it.

How to Treat Your Pricing and Customer Acquisition Model Right

Don't overcomplicate your pricing page

Before signing up for a free trial or freemium model, most users check out your pricing page. If it can't pass the five-second test (i.e. users understand which plan is right for them almost immediately) you're hurting customer acquisition. Instead of signing up for your free offer, they'll bounce.

Even if you feel like your pricing page is locked down, consider combating objections on your pricing page. Here's how James Gill, CEO of GoSquared, tackles this problem:

It may sound simple, but we send a triggered automatic message to visitors simply saying "Have any questions about our pricing?" when people have been on our pricing page for more than 30 seconds. It's helped us convert 100s of visitors in real-time.

Even if you have a simple pricing plan, you may still run into the trap of giving away too much for free.

Don't create a free plan with no incentive to upgrade.

You are not running a charity. If you're reading this, I'm going to guess that you work at a for-profit business. By offering the majority of your product for free on a freemium model, you reduce the incentive for people to upgrade.

This can be a tough balance. Offering a key feature for free makes your customer acquisition model more powerful—but you'll drain resources, too. This is a common problem for many businesses that first launch a free trial or freemium model. Without data, it's easy to give away too much for free.

As Craig Walker, Founder and CEO at DialPad notes,

> We made our free service almost too good, so we have a lot of very dedicated, very happy free users, and sometimes we have a hard time upselling them because they're like, "Hey, why would I need anything else?" Our stiffest competition is coming from ourselves!

On the other hand, it's also way too easy to give away too little. By doing so, you make it extremely hard for new users to see value in your product—the powerful, fun features are hidden behind closed doors.

If you go too far to one side—if you lose your balance—lots of customers might downgrade, which brings me to my second point.

Don't make it a no-brainer for the majority of your customers to downgrade.

One of the most common questions I get from companies launching a freemium model is "What happens if we give away so much that our paying customers downgrade to a free plan?"

There's no way to avoid this entirely, but you can minimize risk. Look at the number of customers who use only the tools and features you're about to give away for free:

- How many of these paying customers would be a prime fit for your free plan?

- What percentage of these paying customers are you willing to risk losing?

- How many more users do you expect to generate by giving away this free feature?

- Is it worth it for your business to give this feature away for free?

- Does this free feature include a value metric?

Most businesses I've worked with typically have 10–15% of customers at risk of downgrading. And yet, the majority still go ahead with their new pricing. Why? Because although you have the potential to lose 10–15% of your customers, a good portion will use more areas of the product in the future—if you have a solid customer success strategy.

You'll also attract more people into your funnel, which will be an active revenue driver for your business. Are you willing to take a short-term dip in revenue for a long-term gain?

Before we can dive into how to communicate value on your pricing page, I want to explain some of the conventional approaches that SaaS businesses take with pricing.

Four Common Pricing Strategies

When it comes to pricing, this quote from Price Intelligently[21] sums up how most companies approach it:

> Some will say you should go with your gut. Others say that you should go with your gut, then double it. Either way, it seems most pricing advice out there is gastrointestinal-based rather than brain-based.

So, how do you pick the right pricing strategy? Let's explore the four main options for SaaS businesses.

1. Best-Judgement Pricing

This is much like it sounds. You and your team decide your price based on what you think is reasonable. Having a low sales month? Discount. Making too many sales but can't support new customers? Increase prices. It's simple supply and demand.

Best judgement pricing is the *least* effective pricing strategy because you rely on the collective experience of your team, and you make assumptions about what your buyer values and is willing to pay.

This guessing leads to fewer sales, and—the real killer— it's easy to sell unprofitable products without knowing it. The next best pricing model is cost-plus pricing. At the very least, it'll help sell at a profit.

2. Cost-Plus Pricing

Cost-Plus Pricing works when you calculate the cost of selling and delivering the product, then add a profit margin on top. Now we're making money!

The problem with cost-plus pricing for SaaS businesses is that although you could charge $100 per customer each month, your marginal costs of supporting a new customer may be quite low (e.g. $1–5).

If you use cost-plus pricing, you're most likely saying goodbye to the majority of your business' profit potential. No Ferrari for you. But, maybe your competitors have a Ferrari, so you assume what they're doing must be working.

3. Competitor-Based Pricing

Competitor-based pricing benchmarks your pricing based on their data. It's relatively simple if your competitors publicly show their pricing. Even if your competitors don't show their pricing, you can be a bit sneaky and find it.

Here's the problem: Regardless of how you conjure up your competitor's pricing info, you're assuming that you sell to the exact same customer who has the exact same problem that you can solve with your exact same product. Now, if you just hired a team in India to replicate another SaaS service, maybe that's true. But in most cases, it's not.

The other interesting part about competitor-based pricing is that you're assuming that your competitor has done their customer and pricing research, which isn't necessarily the case. In fact, ProfitWell did a study and claims that seven out of ten companies do not do their pricing research.[22] There's a lot of guessing out there!

So, although your competitor might have a Ferrari today, they could be trading it in for a pedal-bike tomorrow. You don't know. Why bank your livelihood on someone else's guessing game? If you're serious about pricing your SaaS business the right way, you need to deploy a value-based pricing model.

4. *Value-Based Pricing*

Value-based pricing bases your price on the value you provide. You determine this by taking into account how prospects value your product. A significant benefit of value-based pricing—and, as part of the process, doing pricing and customer research—is that you'll learn what to include in each package.

This approach to pricing helps you understand what your customers truly want and which features to develop.

Which Pricing Approach Will You Take?

As Patrick Campbell, CEO of ProfitWell, says,

> Each of these pricing strategies has its place in business. If you're running a gas station, you're probably cost-plus pricing. If you are in the ultra-competitive retail space, pricing in line with competitors will be close to the price the market can sustain.

> But in SaaS, the only viable option is value-based. Your SaaS company exists to offer value to your customers. By finding out how much they are willing to pay for your product and what features they want to see you develop, then you will be able to not only give customers what they want, but you'll also be able to attract and retain these customers better. All while making more profit.

Now, I'm curious, which pricing model are you going to choose? It's value-based pricing, right?

I'll take that as a "Yes." Great choice. Let's figure out how much you should charge.

How to Determine Your Price

Given that seven out of ten *guess* what price to charge their customers, it's absolutely worthwhile to do the hard work—to figure out what your product is really worth to your customers.

To determine your price, go through both options below:

- **Option 1: Pricing Economic Value Analysis.** How you can use an economic value analysis to come close to the perceived value of your product. This analysis is perfect if you're just starting out, don't have a lot of data, or don't have buy-in to talk to your customers about pricing.

- **Option 2: Market and Customer Research.** A battle-tested method used by Simon Kucher & Partners, Openview, and Price Intelligently to figure out your customers' willingness to pay. If you have lots of customers, I'd recommend choosing this option. It's more accurate than an economic value analysis.

Jump to the option that best suits your business, or read both.

Option 1: Pricing Economic Value Analysis

Any techniques/strategies that don't take the customer into consideration as the main input when developing a price is not going to get you close to where you need to be. If you think creating your SaaS pricing strategy is a function of Finance, Accounting, Operations, or even Sales... you're doing it wrong. **That means anyone who comes up with a price for their app (or for your app) as the result of a spreadsheet function is doing it wrong**.

- Lincoln Murphy,[23] Customer Success Expert

And yet, most businesses whip up a new pricing model in a spreadsheet without talking to a single customer. To avoid bombing with your new pricing model, break down your customer's perceived value across the three core outcomes your product solves for: functional, emotional, and social.

Functional Outcome: The core tasks that customers want to get done

From a functional perspective, what does your product help people do? Typically, a functional outcome breaks down into factors such as incremental revenue, reduced cost, reduced risk, or time savings.

In my experience, many SaaS founders have a good handle on the functional outcome of their product—they often created their solution to solve for their own problem. For instance, Marko Savic, the founder of Funnelcake,[24] started his company after crunching numbers—for more than a week each quarter—to figure out his team's marketing and sales performance.

Given the time investment and importance of "knowing your numbers" for marketing and sales, Marko decided to create a software solution to help businesses stay on track from lead to revenue.

There are a couple of ways to estimate how valuable Marko's software tool is to a buyer.

Let's say Marko was paid $80,000 per year at his previous company. One week of crunching numbers cost Marko's former employer $1,538 per quarter, or more than $6,153 each year.

After Marko finalized these reports, he'd learn which marketing channels to stop investing in, what deals were worth pursuing, and how to double lead-to-revenue conversion rates. If Marko's previous employer was a $1,000,000 business, these findings could quickly help the company grow top-line revenue by 10%. That's $100,000!

From a functional perspective, Marko's tool can drive over $106,153 in value each year for a $1,000,000 business. But, that just scrapes the surface of total value.

Emotional Outcome: How customers want to feel—or avoid feeling—as a result of executing the core functional job

Do people really like to "crunch the numbers"? If you were a creative director like Marko, you didn't. It was that one quarterly activity you hated. You did it only because the output was so essential.

If you were Marko and I told you that you no longer had to crunch the numbers—that you could get them with the same effort it takes to flip on a damn light switch—how much would that be worth to you? Would you pay $5 or $50,000 for that peace of mind? Let's play it conservative and say we'd pay $4,000 for peace of mind. That's just $1,000 each quarter.

Now, you may think, "I'm in the world of B2B. People don't buy like that. They make rational decisions purely on an ROI basis." But you're wrong. B2B buyers may, in fact, be even *more* emotional than their B2C counterparts. A survey[25] of more than 3,000 B2B buyers by Google and CEB revealed that:

> Not only did the B2B brands drive more emotional connections than B2C brands, but they weren't even close. Of the hundreds of B2C brands that Motista has studied, most have emotional connections with between 10% and 40% of consumers. Meanwhile, of the nine B2B brands we studied, seven surpassed the 50% mark.

Talia Wolf, CEO of GetUplift, explains the broader context:[26]

> We all invest our money in products, experiences, and services that make us feel a certain way – loved, safe, appreciated, part of a community, strong or perhaps just better than others. Emotions play a key role in our decision making process both online and offline and in order to truly grow your business you have to start understanding your customers and their decision making process better. - Talia Wolf, CEO at GetUplift[27]

Although we buy while looking for functional *and* emotional outcomes, most people forget about social outcomes.

Social Outcome: How customers want to be perceived by others

Instead of a chart cobbled together in Microsoft Excel, Marko's software helps you put together brilliant, professional reports that you can show to your executive team.

You aren't seen as the Excel guru anymore (which is replaceable). Because you didn't spend an entire week crunching numbers, you had the time to put together a plan of attack for how you're going to hit your targets. Your executive team is amazed by your insights into the business and your detailed plan. You've become invaluable. You even get a promotion. Fancy that!

As the buyer of Marko's software, what's that worth to you? It's extremely hard to place a number on what a promotion is worth to someone, or how much it's worth to feel like a "professional" during a presentation.

Given how hard it is to distill the value of a social outcome, I like to leave it as the cherry on the top. We should always over deliver. One of the most powerful ways to do is to make the customer look like a badass for choosing your product.

How to complete the value economic analysis

If we combine the functional and emotional value of Marko's software, that's over $110,000 in value each year for a $1,000,000 business. Not bad. But, how do you determine your price? Lincoln Murphy offers one solution:[28]

> So a very good way to determine your price is to follow the 10x Rule. "We charge this much because our customers get at least 10x that much value." If I sell something for $100, I want to provide at least $1,000 in value to them... at least. All we can do is get it AS RIGHT AS POSSIBLE out of the gate and understand that pricing is not a "set it and forget it" function, but – just as your overall Marketing Strategy is

ever-evolving and changing with market forces, market feedback, etc.

If we apply the 10x rule to Marko's software, we divide by ten. Our customers will often be more than willing to pay $11,000 annually for our solution.

To refine this pricing model, continually ask your customers about the value they get from the product. If you use an outcome-based value metric tied to revenue, you'll quickly uncover how much value your product provides. However, if you use a functional value metric or feature differentiation, you need to talk to customers regularly to find out how valuable they find your solution.

Now, if you'd like a more scientific way to understand what to charge your customers, do market research.

Option 2: Market and Customer Research

Basing your pricing on market and customer research is one of the best ways to understand how much your customer is willing to pay for your product or service. The model I'm going to share with you is based on the Van Westendorp Price Sensitivity Meter.[29] (I'm not sure how to pronounce "Westendorp," so we can just refer to this as the "Van West Model" from here on out.)

This is the same model that pricing experts at ProfitWell, Openview, and Simon-Kucher rely on to help SaaS businesses nail their pricing. (I'm not sharing their proprietary method. This is simply one part of their framework.) One of the most significant benefits of using the Van West Model is that it will help you find an acceptable price *range*.

Finding an acceptable price range is especially important because we want to avoid two disastrous consequences:

1. We set our price too high and lose out on the majority of sales.

2. We set our price too low and lose out on the majority of profits (while also hurting our brand, which appears "cheap").

You can figure out the acceptable price range in three steps.

Step 1: Prepare Questions to Ask

In the Van West Model, you need to ask four questions to discover your ideal price range. You want to know at what point people find your product too expensive or cheap:

1. **Too Expensive.** At what price point would you consider [our product] to be so expensive that you would not consider buying it?

2. **Expensive.** At what price point would you consider [our product] so expensive that, while not out of the question, you would give it some thought before buying?

3. **Bargain.** At what price point would you consider [our product] to be a great deal for the money?

4. **Too Cheap.** At what price point would you consider [our product] so inexpensive that you would feel the quality couldn't be excellent?

Each question helps pinpoint where your pricing should be. The more customers you ask, the closer you'll get to finding your acceptable price range. Kyle Poyar, VP of Market Strategy at Openview, suggests an alternative way[30] of using the Van West Model:

While the proper technique involves four categories of questions, I focus on two: what the buyer considers an "acceptable" price (good value for the money) and at what point the price would start to get "expensive" (they'd have to think twice about buying it).

If the price you were thinking of is below what an average buyer considers to be "acceptable," then you're leaving money on the table. If the price is above what an average prospect considers "expensive", then you'll probably face adoption hurdles and need to work especially hard at proving the value.

In short, if you want to follow Poyar's advice, you can find your acceptable price range by asking just two questions:

1. What would you consider to be an "acceptable" price (good value for the money) for [our product]?

2. When would [our product] seem "expensive" (they'd have to think twice about buying it)?

If you don't have a lot of customers, I'd recommend using Kyle's method. You'll get more people to answer your questions, which brings us to our next topic. How do we get people to answer these questions in the first place?

Step 2: How to Ask

The ideal people to ask are your customers and Product Qualified Leads (PQLs). As for *how* you ask, there are two main ways:

1. Survey tools (Typeform, SurveyMonkey);

2. Interviews.

Either option has advantages and disadvantages. For instance, you're unlikely to schedule an interview with a customer to ask them only four questions about pricing. I would frame interviews as a way to improve the product and better understand customers' needs. This way, you're not pitching it as a pricing interview, and you can ask other valuable questions.

If you decide to go down the survey route, you can make it easy for survey respondents to pick a price range by displaying multiple options.

Willingness to Pay	$100	$300	$500	$700	$900	$1100
At what price point would you consider [our product] to be so expensive that you would not consider buying it? [Too Expensive]						X
At what price point would you consider [our product] starting to get expensive, so that, while not out of the question, you would give it some thought before buying? [Expensive]				X		

At what price point would you consider [our product] to be an excellent deal for the money? [Bargain]		X				
At what price point would you consider [our product] so inexpensive that you would feel the quality couldn't be excellent? [Too Cheap]	X					

Giving survey participants a range of responses will improve your completion rate. But your results may be off if you don't know the reasonable price range for your product. Be careful when picking a price range, or just ask people to give you an exact number for each question. You'll get fewer survey completions, but your results will be more accurate. Once you have answers, it's time to do some digging.

Step 3: Crunch the Numbers

With the Van West Model, your X-axis includes the prices people said they'd be willing to pay. The Y-axis has the percentage of people who selected each price range.

Pay attention to the points of intersection. Between the "Not a Bargain" and "Too Cheap" price ranges, the Point of Marginal Cheapness (PMC) shows where people consider our product cheap. Don't charge less than that.

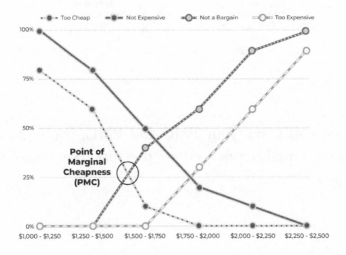

At the intersection of "Too Expensive" and "Not Expensive," we find the Point of Marginal Expensiveness (PME). This is an excellent place to be—the point where people start to consider our product expensive.

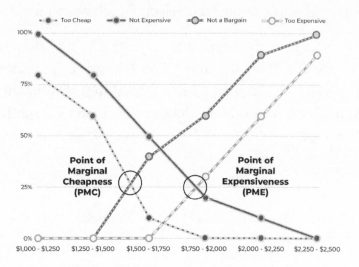

Once you know your PMC and PME, you've found your acceptable price range: the space between both points.

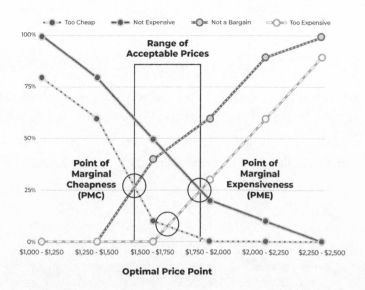

As Price Intelligently notes, you may uncover more than one ideal price range: "Just as with feature analysis, you can then break these numbers down by buyer personas, finding the optimum price point for each potential customer." I'd go even further. Break this down by the plan each participant uses to determine the willingness to pay for each package you offer.

Now that we know how to find our acceptable price range, it's time to transfer everything we've learned onto the pricing page.

What Should You Put on Your Pricing Page?

Putting together a pricing page doesn't have to be complicated. You need four elements to make it work:

1. Value Metric;

2. Willingness to pay for all packages;

3. Valued features;

4. Demographic Information.

In the previous chapter, we talked about the importance of value metrics. For instance, if you're Wistia, your value metric could be the number of videos uploaded or video views. We're going to put your value metric to good use.

If you have a functional- or outcome-based value metric, it must be a core component of your pricing page.

The willingness to pay is based on market research we've already done. The valued features is a tricky section. Which features should we include with each plan?

According to Kyle Poyar,[31] there are only three main categories:

1. **Leaders** "are the hamburger in your McDonald's value meal; they are what everyone wants and comes to you to buy. These must be included in all packages."

2. **Fillers** "are the fries and coke. They are seen as nice-to-have and sweeten the deal. Customers will cherry pick fillers when sold a la carte, and so a bundle helps drive uptake and a higher average revenue per user (ARPU)."

3. **Bundle killers** "are the coffee of your value meal. Few people want a value meal with a burger, fries, coke AND a coffee, and adding coffee to the value meal might even turn people off from buying entirely because they'd end up with more than they need. There will be a handful of caffeine-starved customers who do want the coffee, though, and they can purchase it a la carte outside of the value meal."

Lastly, where does demographic information fit into a pricing page? Often, savvy businesses will name the pricing tier after each of their personas or give it a similar nickname to signify the type of buyer who regularly purchases that plan.

This serves two purposes:

1. It allows your audience to self-segment quicker.

2. It helps you prioritize the features and benefits that are most valuable to the target audience.

Once you have all these components, you can put together your pricing page.

At this point, you should understand your value and how to communicate it to the market. You're ready for the next challenge: Getting incredibly good at delivering on that value.

CHAPTER 10

Deliver on Your Value

Do you have a friend or family member who exaggerates their experiences? I know I do. After listening to them for a while, do you find it hard to trust what they say? I can hear you say "yes" from a mile away.

The same thing applies when selling software. What we promise in our marketing and sales is the **perceived value.** What we deliver in our product is the **experienced value.** Ideally, the perceived value aligns with the experienced value.

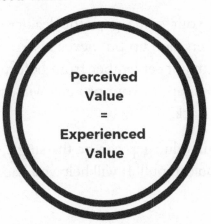

Everyone is happy in this scenario—what we signed up for does exactly what we envisioned. But this is rarely the case. Most companies struggle with overpromising and under-delivering.

It's one reason why product-led businesses are booming. People want to "try before they buy" and *experience* your value proposition. If you keep your word, it's a great way to build trust and sell your product. If you fail to deliver, your user experiences a nasty value gap.

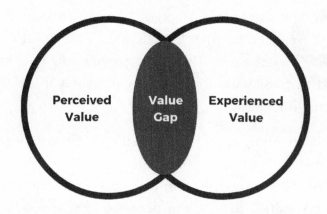

The bigger your value gap, the leakier your funnel. You'll see users sign up but never return to your product. As you might remember from before, 40–60% of users who sign up for your product will use it once and never come back.

Tackling your value gap can be the single, most profitable lever you can pull. It will help you launch and build a free trial or freemium model that (actually) turns users into customers. There are three main reasons why value gaps are so prominent in the SaaS industry:

1. Your product has serious ability debt;

2. You don't understand why your customers buy;

3. You overpromise what the solution is capable of.

Before launching a product-led arm of your business, declare war on your value gap. You'll be in a much better position to create a product that can reduce your CACs, acquire more customers, and turn non-paying users into customers.

The Three Value Gaps You Need to Crush

Value Gap 1: Ability Debt

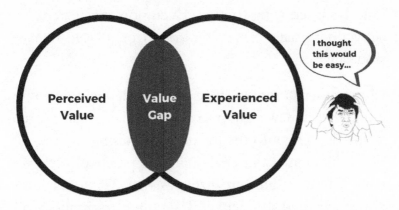

Ability debt is the price you pay every time your user fails to accomplish a key outcome in your product.

Richard Kipp, Chief Product Officer at Grow, uses a spaghetti analogy. If your company was a restaurant, the outcome people value is food. People are coming into your business expecting to buy a hot plate of spaghetti, and then they get ushered by the customer service team into the kitchen with all the tools and features to make it yourself.

Your sales and marketing can't go out and tell people, "Hey, we have hot and ready spaghetti for just $5!" and when the customers come, they see that there is no dining room and no hot and ready spaghetti and "oh, by the way, you need to bring your own spaghetti, ground beef, sauce, olive oil, onions, and garlic. Also, you've got to know how to use all of these tools if you really want spaghetti. This is where churn happens.

To chip away at your ability debt, you need to be ruthless about reducing friction. Even non-trivial steps like activation emails can crater your free-to-paid conversion rate.

Christopher Gimmer, the CEO of Snappa, initially required every new signup to activate their email address before logging into the product. Requiring users to activate their email address is standard practice. However, what Gimmer didn't realize was that 27% of signups never activated their email. Users never saw the product.

In less than a week, Christopher's team removed the email activation step. If Snappa's current free-to-paid conversion rate held up, this one change would net a six-figure ARR outcome. When the results came in, they showed a 20% boost in MRR.

This is one of countless examples. But conquering ability debt will never go away. As Kipp notes, "You need to evolve your technology to a point where people can get hot and ready spaghetti without having to learn how to use the kitchen. As you remove pain and friction from your user's experience of attaining their valued objective, your total addressable market grows."

When you first launch a free trial or freemium model, you will inevitably have some severe ability debt. It's expected. However, to improve your experience, you continuously need to look for ways to improve.

Ask yourself these questions while going through your product experience:

- Does the first product experience lead to a specific, relevant, meaningful "quick win"?

- Do tooltips and hotspots spur meaningful action in the product, not just point at buttons?

- Do social and directional cues indicate high-value behaviors?

- Are key task completions indicated with a success state, such as Mailchimp's famous high-five?

- Are all unnecessary points of friction and distraction removed from critical workflows?

Each question helps you spot opportunities to reduce or eliminate ability debt. You can ask *yourself* infinite questions, but eventually, you need to talk to your customers. In Part III, we'll dive deeper into how to reduce ability debt and help users experience your value proposition sooner. For now, get crystal clear on what you promise users when they sign up.

Value Gap 2: You Don't Understand Why People Buy Your Product.

If you don't know where someone wants to go, you can't help them get there. Until you know what your users are trying to accomplish in your product, you'll lead them to mountaintops they never wanted to climb.

Let's say our friends at PayPal have a goal to generate 100,000 leads this month. The PayPal team might use Google Ads, Facebook, SEO, and remarketing to hit the lead target. Each marketing channel needs to get the PayPal team closer to hitting their lead generation outcome of 100,000 leads this month.

Since we understand the outcome of the PayPal team, we know that our product needs to help them generate leads. However, if we don't understand the outcome PayPal is looking to solve for, what's stopping us from forcing the PayPal team to set up a branding campaign?

Once we know the main outcome that our user is looking for, we can catapult them into the area of the product that is most relevant to them. Canva, a simple visual editor, does a brilliant job at shortcutting the time it takes to achieve a particular outcome in their product.

For instance, just type "how to make a poster" in Google and click on the Canva link. Once you click on the call to action, you're directed to register for an account. Once you do, you're immediately brought to the poster section of the product. In less than a minute, you're able to select a poster from thousands of beautiful templates and edit the design you choose with ease.

When it comes to onboarding, most businesses walk you through the entire product but bring you no closer to achieving a meaningful outcome in the product. That isn't too different than inviting your friends over to your house for dinner and, when they show up, you show them around the house but forget to give them anything to eat. Oops!

Although you might have a great house, your friends came for dinner. Same goes for your product. Although people come to your product and expect it to be neat and tidy, they're really there for the main outcome.

When you understand *why* people use your product, you can catapult them to the right destination. If you don't know the primary outcome behind why people use your product, you're growing your business on hard mode. **What outcome does your product help people with?** Is it lead generation? Is it getting more fit?

This may sound straightforward, but many businesses don't know the main outcome that people want to achieve in their product. As a result, they unknowingly force unnecessary steps onto users during onboarding. It's easy to do. If you don't understand your product's value, what's stopping you from showing unnecessary features that *might* be helpful?

To reduce your value gap, set the right expectations.

Value Gap 3: You Suck At Communicating Your Value

If someone signs up for your product thinking that it's a live-chat solution when it's actually a telemarketing solution, you're going to confuse users. Even if you're clear on what your solution does, you can misinform users about how long it takes to do it—companies often promote how fast their solution gets results when, in reality, it takes a lot more time.

This hurts your brand and increases the chances of new users leaving your initial product experience. Delivering on your value and reducing your value gap starts and ends with helping people. There are no shortcuts or magic tools.

Before diving into *how* to deliver on your value, let's identify the people *within* your own company whom you need to convince.

Whom do you need to convince to launch a product-led strategy?

There's nothing more disappointing than this scenario: You put in countless hours creating a compelling business case to launch or optimize a free trial or freemium model—then your product or sales team shuts you down.

A student from my Product-Led Growth course[32] ran into this issue. He wanted to optimize his company's free-trial sign-up page by reducing the number of required form fields, but the sales team demanded that they keep all ten fields. It took him three months to convince the sales director to reduce the number of fields.

This scenario isn't uncommon. In my experience, it's typically your Chief Technology Officer (CTO) or VP of Sales who shuts you down. That makes a bit more sense: The CTO needs to ensure his team is keeping pace with the product roadmap; the VP of Sales needs to meet revenue targets. If your free-trial experiment gets in the way of their agendas, they can quickly shut you down.

Launching a free trial or freemium model also requires development time (at the expense of product feature roll-out) and cannibalizes demo requests (at the expense of hitting sales targets). To de-risk your free-trial launch, you need to sell your product and sales team on why a free trial will help them grow.

This is, of course, much easier said than done, but, in my experience, it's most important to get the CEO onboard with the vision. If you can do that, it's much easier to convince other leaders within the organization to give a free-trial or freemium launch a shot. If you're the CEO and reading this, you're already one step ahead of the pack.

One of the easiest ways to launch a free trial or freemium model is to launch an MVP version to "test the waters" and see if it's worth your team's time and investment. This whole process can take less than 24 hours.

Although you could start by launching a freemium model, I'd urge you to shelve that idea for now. Regardless of whether you're using a differentiated, dominant, or disruptive strategy, you need to start with a free trial. Once your free trial is proven to convert, you can consider freemium.

How to launch a free trial in 24 hours

Launching a free trial doesn't have to be a three- to six-month process in which your engineering team rehauls the product and you invest hundreds of thousands of dollars for an experiment.

You can launch a free trial in 24 hours—even under an hour. All you need to do is pull out your credit card and pay me $5,000. I'm kidding. In all seriousness, you need to do two things:

1. **Update your "Request a Demo" CTA to a "Request a Free Trial" CTA.**

2. **On your demo landing page, change the text from "demo" to "free trial."**

Voila. You have a free trial. Once someone signs up for your free trial—which should be anytime now—they're going to expect to be able to use your product. (Shocker.) Instead of giving them the keys, book a meeting with them. (Use Calendly or a similar alternative on the thank-you page after someone requests a "trial." You'll thank me later when people book meetings with you!)

In your first meeting with the new trialer, do several things:

1. **Qualify them as you usually would.** If they're a good fit, let them dive into using the product right away. If not, well, no hard feelings pal.

2. **Ask them about the primary outcome they want to achieve with the product.** Record these calls and use video so that you can see their body language—they might not tell you that your product is confusing as hell, but a fiery eye roll as you explain how "simple" it is will.

3. **Watch the trialer try to achieve an outcome in the product.** Ask your trialer to share their screen. (I recommend Zoom.) Do not show your trialer how to do everything. You want to

see your trialer struggle. If you don't let them struggle, the customer won't remember how to accomplish that particular outcome, nor will you learn about your product's shortcomings. Typically you have to pay for user testing. In this scenario, you're getting it for free. (You're welcome!)

When you're running onboarding sessions, really seek out the top three outcomes. Knowing them will help you eventually catapult people into areas of the product that matter to them.

After your first onboarding session, here are the next steps:

1. Write down the key outcome(s) that someone wanted to accomplish.

Put this in a spreadsheet or somewhere you won't lose it. Each time you onboard a new trialer, add to this list. Eventually, you'll learn which outcomes are most important. If you're looking for an "Aha!" moment, you'll get it—in real time.

These key outcomes will guide your marketing and initial onboarding, but that's getting a little ahead of ourselves. For now, focus on helping your user. Things do *not* need to scale at this point. You can create trial accounts manually, set up APIs for integrations, and even give users your personal cell phone so that they can call you in the middle of the night (kidding).

Over time, you'll find out what needs to be automated by the sheer number of requests and how painful they are for your team to manage.

2. Focus on where you need to offer a helping hand.

People will find it challenging to accomplish critical outcomes in your product, especially if you've been a sales-led company that's now trying to transition to a product-led organization.[33] That's okay. You just have a lot of ability debt to chip away.

When reviewing onboarding sessions, take special notes of when people mess up. This is an opportunity for you to improve your product experience or add a helpful tooltip.

3. Lastly, clear the damn path.

You're going to have garbage that prevents users from experiencing a key outcome in your product. When it comes to your onboarding, every step that doesn't help your user experience a meaningful outcome should be removed.

Just like in the Snappa.com example I shared earlier—in which an email activation step kept 27% of new signups from ever logging in—you need to challenge each step. By removing the email activation step from the initial onboarding experience, Snappa boosted their MRR by 20%. Removing one unnecessary step from your onboarding may not have such a monumental impact, but it just might!

By challenging each step in your onboarding, you'll create a superhighway for your users to accomplish a key outcome in your product. In Part III, I'll share a framework that streamlines your onboarding and helps your users become successful.

Now that we've covered the UCD framework, I want to challenge you. Even if you do a terrible job understanding and communicating your value, there's one thing you can do that will keep your business running smoothly: **Deliver on your value.**

If you can do that one thing, and get consistently better at it, you'll build a strong foundation for your product-led business—as long as you avoid one killer mistake.

CHAPTER 11

The Most Common Mistake that New Product-Led Businesses Make

Most SaaS companies launch their product-led model. Then they never update it. When the executive team calls me and asks why they aren't converting users into customers, I tell them to buy a plant. Seriously.

If they don't water it, it's going to wither and die. If you water the plant and give it sunlight, it'll grow. Everyone knows how the system works. Yet, even though we know what to do, millions of plant still die. Why? **Nobody takes ownership.**

If you hired an employee and told them that their *only* job was to water *one* plant, would that plant get watered? Absolutely. The problem is that most businesses don't appoint a person or team to take ownership, nor do they give that person the resources or time it takes to thrive.

Is it your marketing, sales, customer success, or product team's responsibility to update the product-led model? If you have to think before you can answer the question, you don't have the right people or process in place to optimize your product-led engine.

Who do you need to run a successful product-led engine?

Before you identify *who* you need on your team, let's go see if you need to hire anyone new. Here are your options:

1. **Trial and error.** This option can work if you're self-funded, but it can take a long time to build a high-converting product-led model, and the likelihood of switching back to "the old way" of doing things is high. I went down this route at Vidyard,[34] and believe me: It's like a magnet is drawing you back to a sales-led model.

2. **Hire the dream team.** This option can work if the stakes are high and you don't have enough time; however, it has downsides. You will, no doubt, spend lots of time recruiting, training, and getting your new team up to speed. This burden alone can consume a full quarter. Not to mention, finding people with relevant experi-

ence is hard—these people are in high demand.

3. **Train your team.** This option is the fastest way to get your product-led model up and running. Think about it: Your current employees are already familiar with your product, know your customers, and (hopefully) want to see your customers succeed. When consulting, I've been able to teach teams that are completely new to Product-Led Growth and be able to see incredible results in weeks, not months.

Now, don't go out and train everyone on your team right away. Put together a small tiger team. On this team, you need these seven people (if you're a small startup, you can merge some of these positions together):

1. Developer;

2. User Experience Designer;

3. Product Manager (someone to lead the project);

4. Customer Success Rep;

5. Digital Marketer/Inside Sales;

6. CEO;

7. CPO or CTO.

If you're leading this initiative, pick influential people from each team who have the power to win over others. This tiger team is eventually responsible for building out their own mini-team within your company, so choose carefully.

Once you've put your tiger team together, give them ownership to do whatever it takes to help people become successful with the product. This could include welcoming new free-trial users via snail mail, calling every sign-up, or even creating short personalized videos to show each user around.

At this point, it doesn't matter if it scales. All that matters is putting a team in place that desperately wants users to succeed. Once you have the right team in place—even if it's just a list of people you think would be a great fit—take the first small step. Ask these people (or your entire company) to send you ideas on how to improve the product-led model. Ask for answers by the end of the week.

It will take less than five minutes to send out an email, and you'll receive brilliant ideas to implement in a matter of days. Note that the biggest bottlenecks to optimizing your product-led model have nothing to do with your product—it all comes down to having the right team and process in place.

With that team in place, the next step is to develop an ongoing optimization process.

Part III

Ignite Your Growth Engine

CHAPTER 12

Develop an Optimization Process

At the Product-Led Institute, we developed the "Triple A" sprint, which focuses on rapidly identifying problems, building solutions, and measuring impact. The process follows a one-month sprint cycle and consists of three "A's":

1. Analyze;

2. Ask;

3. Act.

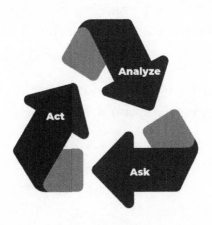

The Triple A sprint gives you a way to build a sustainable growth process and can be used by any team in your business.

Still, if you have a bad product, no optimization will deliver rocketship growth. Just because you put sprinkles on a turd does not transform it into a brownie. At the end of the day, it's still shit.

On the other hand, if you have a good product that customers love, you'll see a monumental shift if you go through a Triple A sprint each month.

I've seen companies apply this same framework and go from $500,000 ARR to $1 million ARR in less than 12 months. It works. Best of all, it's not hard to implement. Start by analyzing your business.

The First "A": Analyze

As Romain Lapeyre,[35] CEO of Gorgias, states, "In order to build a growth machine for your business, you need to analyze your inputs and outputs." Until you know the inputs (e.g. trade shows, advertising, email marketing) that drive desired outputs (e.g. ARR, customers, MRR), you won't build a sustainable business.

If you're not sure which inputs drive the outputs you want in your business, you need to start analyzing your business.

Inputs
- Trade shows
- Advertising
- Email Campaigns

Outputs
- Customers
- ARR
- ARPU

Where to Start Analyzing Your Business

Create a recurring calendar notification to remind yourself to analyze your previous month's results on the first workday of each new month. Block off one or two hours so that you'll have the time to do a thorough job. You'll get into a rhythm of analysis.

Start measuring your outputs. Outputs are a reliable indicator of whether you're doing the right thing—they don't lie. Let's dive into the right outputs to track.

Which Outputs Should You Track?

One of the beautiful things about a SaaS business is that you can analyze almost anything. This amount of insight is incredible—until it isn't. With access to countless metrics, it's easy to obsess over email opens or bounce rates. Although these metrics can be tracked, they don't tell you much.

Did your high bounce rate lead customers to churn? Or did it hurt signups? Although a high bounce rate can absolutely contribute to those problems, we still don't know the root cause. By looking at outputs, we can quickly analyze the area of our business that most requires our attention. That way, we know which areas to troubleshoot.

In a product-led business, these are the macro outputs you need to track:

- Number of signups;

- Number of upgrades;

- Average Revenue Per User (ARPU);

- Customer Churn;

- ARR;

- MRR.

These outputs don't lie, and they're are easy to find. If you compare these outputs over the course of the last 12 months, you'll quickly identify the area of your business that's hurting the most.

Once we know the outputs, we can ask questions to identify the inputs that get us closer to our dream business.

The Second "A": Ask

To optimize any business, you need to ask three questions:

1. Where Do You Want to Go?

Some businesses use a North Star Metric to symbolize

this focus, while others pick a revenue number. How you break down your business' goals is not what this book is about.

If you really have no idea what your organization's goals are, you should read *Measure What Matters*[36] by John Doerr. It lays the foundation for how to prioritize the metrics that matter in your business and work to hit them across your entire team.

As an example, let's say we're a $10 million ARR SaaS business that has a live-chat solution. Our numeric objective is to hit $15 million ARR in the next 12 months. I'm all for setting ambitious goals, but please do not just "wing it" when it comes to figuring out what to do next. To get your business closer to where you want to go, you need to know which levers to pull.

2. Which Levers Can You Pull to Get There?

As I'm writing this book, I'm taking a motorbike course. As a newbie, I'm constantly making mistakes. I'll shift down a gear when going fast, and my bike will screech and hiss in anger. I'll hold down the clutch while accelerating only to hear my engine roar and feel my bike slow. I'll use the front brake while slowing around a corner, toppling my bike onto me—an anti-climatic end that risks embarrassment more than injury.

Knowing which levers to pull is important for business or motorbikes. What's also true is that there are multiple ways to get the same output. To stop a motorbike, you can use the front, back, or engine brake. Or just drive into the nearest lake. Each of these braking systems achieves the desired output.

It's the same when it comes to your business. According to Jay Abraham's multiplier perspective, there are three levers you can pull for growth:

1. Multiplier 1: Churn;

2. Multiplier 2: Average revenue per user (ARPU);

3. Multiplier 3: Number of customers.

When I talk to executives at product-led businesses, most focus almost exclusively on increasing the number of customers; however, when it comes to increasing ARPU or decreasing churn, I hear crickets. This is a huge missed opportunity. According to Tomasz Tunguz,[37] "A healthy growing SaaS company with -5% churn has 73% higher revenue than one with 5% churn."

If our goal is to increase our revenue, why is everyone looking at the customer count? Drew Sanocki, former CMO at Teamwork.com, found that decreasing his churn rate by 30%, increasing ARPU by 30%, and increasing total customers by only 30% increased LTV *by over 100%*.

Breaking down your business by three levers lets you quickly identify which levers will help you your business grow fastest. Unless you're just starting out, reducing churn and increasing ARPU will almost always have the biggest impact. Once you nail your churn and ARPU, you can start multiplying your business with each additional customer.

Here's the multiplier formula you can use:

Churn > ARPU > # Customers

Want to see how it works? Fill in the graph below to see which lever will have the biggest impact on your business.

Metric	Scenario A	Scenario B	Difference
Customer Count	Current (e.g. 1,000)		0%
ARPU	Current (e.g. 100)		0%
Annual Churn Rate	Current (e.g. 20%)		0%
ARR	Current (e.g. $80,000)		0%

Once you've identified the top lever, it's time to brainstorm which inputs will kick your business into high gear.

3. Which Inputs Should We Invest In?

Once we've found where to focus our Triple A sprint,

we can figure out which inputs we should add to or subtract from the mix. If we use the right inputs, our business and outputs will grow.

If we make a mistake and use the wrong inputs, our business will become stagnant or decline.

To help you find the right inputs, recall the UCD framework and why companies fail:

1. You don't understand your value.

2. You aren't communicating your value well enough.

3. You aren't delivering on your value fast enough.

That's it. Just three potential issues.

Ask yourself: Which part of your business is underperforming? Brainstorm potential inputs to run experiments. This is easier said than done, but don't overthink it. If you're struggling with low signups, do customer research to understand the value your buyer perceives. Then, communicate that value to them.

If you're struggling with low upgrade rates, work on delivering your value. Cut out every piece of onboarding that doesn't deliver on your value. As Samuel Hullick cautioned, "People don't use software simply because they have tons of spare time and find clicking buttons enjoyable."

One way to find opportunities to improve the buying experience is to buy your product once a month. You'll quickly spot easy improvements. Too often, we set up our onboarding and assume it works without a hitch. (It doesn't.) I've done countless user onboarding audits and found embarrassing bugs that were cratering free-to-paid conversion rates. Anyone could've spotted these bugs.

Compile a list of items that could improve your product experience. Filter these ideas. *How* you do it doesn't matter as much as *having a defined process*. As Scott Williamson, VP of Product at SendGrid, implored, "Have a consistent prioritization system, so you can compare the value of very different projects, force priority decisions out into the light, and pressure test assumptions."

I use an Input Log[38] as a prioritization system. It helps you track and prioritize every idea that could help your business grow. Then, I use the ICE prioritization method, developed by Sean Ellis, to score each input on three elements:

1. **Impact.** How big of an impact could this input have on an output I want to improve?

2. **Confidence.** How confident am I that this input will improve my output metrics?

3. **Ease.** How easy is it to implement?

Here's an example of what this could look like:

Inputs	Impact	Confidence	Ease	ICE Score
Because we noticed quite a few customers having problems upgrading, we expect that adding an "Upgrade Now" button to the header of our in-app experience will make it easier for users to upgrade their account. We'll measure this by monitoring if the signup-to-paid conversion rate improves.	5	5	3	13

You can use any framework you want; however, if you don't have an existing prioritization system, start with the ICE score framework. It's easy to understand and implement.

Once you've run through the ICE method to filter your ideas, find the one or two opportunities to implement that will have the biggest impact on your business. Now, put those ideas to good use.

The Third "A": Act

Ideas are easy. Execution is everything. As Henry David Thoreau would say, "It's not enough to be busy, so are the ants. The question is, what are we busy about?"

Once you've chosen the one or two ideas you're going to implement this month, all you need to do is launch the idea. Depending on the ease of each project, this could take you and your team a few hours or a few weeks.

If this is your first time going through a Triple A sprint, start small. Get some quick wins under your belt. Typically, this means choosing an input that is easy to implement and has a moderate-to-high estimated impact. Later, you can take bigger swings that require more resources and time. For now, take baby steps.

Kieran Flanagan, VP of Marketing at HubSpot, took a similar approach when helping HubSpot transition from a sales-led to a product-led business.

How HubSpot Experimented Its Way to Freemium Growth

The first step in adding freemium to our go-to market strategy was setting the overarching vision of where we wanted to go. Then, our goal was to run experiments to iterate towards the vision or inform how we needed to evolve the vision.

We set our sights on providing companies from big to small with the right tools to grow. We wanted customers to be able to get started with our marketing, sales, and customer success products for free, and upgrade to different packages as their needs grew. Navigating the associated shift to Product-Led Growth (while still growing 30-40% a year!), hasn't been easy. But it has brought valuable learnings.

Here's the high-level process that worked for our growth team:

- Get wins on the board to build trust with leadership and other teams, such as product and engineering.

- Prioritize growth experiments you can execute quickly to demonstrate results.

- Once you start to see a high-level of test failures or non-results, move on to tackle more complex growth opportunities (take big swings).

- Eventually, tell your CEO you want to test pricing ;-) (take even bigger swings)

If you already work in growth, this process of getting quick wins and laddering up should be familiar.

Putting It All Together: Analyze, Ask, Act

Process beats tactics. Following the Triple A sprint framework puts you on track to grow your business consistently. In a market where, over the last five years, CACs have increased more than 50% while willingness to pay is down 30%, we need to instill a culture of optimization. If we can, we'll pull the right levers and put our business in high gear.

For the rest of Part III, I'm going to break down exactly which inputs you can pull to move the needle on your three main levers:

1. Increase the number of customers;

2. Increase average revenue per user (ARPU);

3. Reduce customer churn.

Depending on which lever you struggle with, I encourage you to jump to the chapter that tackles your most urgent problem. But for now, I want to show you one of my favorite frameworks to turn users into customers. I hope you like bowling!

CHAPTER 13

The Bowling Alley Framework

The Bowling Alley Framework is a powerful on-boarding strategy. I've used it to help brands make millions—without spending a dime more on marketing. What-ever industry you're in, this system can help you nail your onboarding and turn users into customers.

If you haven't played 10-pin bowling before, here's how it works. Ten pins stand in a triangular array 60 feet away from you. Between you and the pins, there's an oiled wooden lane that's 41.5 inches wide. You have a ball a little less than 9 inches in diameter that weighs up to 16 pounds. Your goal is to roll your ball down the lane and knock down as many pins as you can.

Here's the bad news: On the left and right edges of the lane, there are gutters. If your ball falls into the gutter, you won't knock down any pins, which means you don't get any points. To win, you need to knock down as many pins as possible each round.

If you're new to 10-pin bowling, it can be frustrating when your ball goes into the gutter. To fix this, Phil Kinzer invented the concept of "bumper bowling," in which a bumper keeps balls from going into the gutters.

When it comes to increasing your customer base, use bumpers to guide your user to the outcome that your product promises.

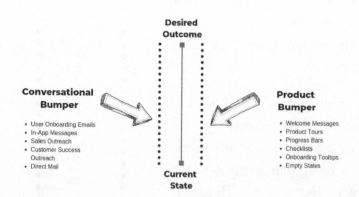

When users get sidetracked or leave the product, it's our duty to bump them back in the right direction. By doing so, we guide users to the part of the product that matters most. You'll prevent users from trailing off and have more users return to the product after the first visit.

To master the Bowling Alley Framework, you need to do three things:

1. Develop your straight line.

2. Create a product bumper.

3. Build a conversational bumper.

One of the best parts about the system is that it's not salesy. It works so well because even a complete newbie can get a strike. This is crucial. As Richard Kipp, CPO at Grow, reminds us, "As you remove pain and friction from your user's experience of attaining their valued objective, your total addressable market grows."

One of the best ways to remove pain and friction is to develop a straight-line onboarding experience.

Why You Need a Straight Line

A straight line is the shortest distance to get from Point A to Point B. Unlike a sales-led organization, in which the goal is to take people from Point A to Point B *in a sales cycle*, we want to take people from Point A to Point B *in their lives*. This is done by letting users try before they buy and doing everything we can to help them experience the value of our product.

The problem, however, is that most users never make it to Point B—that promised land where they experience the value of your product. Why? Most often, we don't know the desired outcome people are looking for, the reason they signed up to use your product.

Take Canva, a simple graphics editor, as an example. You can use the product to create posters, cards, presentations—you name it. Given the incredible number of use-cases, Canva created a web page that shows exactly how to create a poster. On this page, you simply click the call to action to create a poster, and within seconds you're editing a poster in the product.

By understanding the problems people were searching to solve (e.g. how to make a poster) and customizing the onboarding experience to help users solve them, Canva cut their time-to-value in half.

As you can see, knowing your users' intent behind using your product helps us catapult them to the areas where they can experience value as soon as possible. If we can do that one thing—and get consistently better at it—we'll eventually increase the number of free users that turn into paying customers.

By bringing our users to the promised land and delivering on our value, the next logical step for them is to convert to paying customer. Lincoln Murphy of Sixteen Ventures explains: "You'll get that 'they convert to a paying customer' outcome you want, by focusing on the outcome they want."

This sounds fine and dandy. But how do you develop your straight line? How do you help users achieve their desired outcomes in a fraction of the time? You can do this by:

1. Mapping out the path.

2. Labeling every checkpoint.

3. Developing your straight line.

To get the most out of this book, complete these three steps with me. Pull out a pen and paper or open your laptop. Let's get started!

Map Out the Path

In my experience, well over 30% of required user onboarding steps are rubbish. (Yes, yours, too.) Tell me if this sounds familiar. There are form fields that you don't *really* need to ask people when signing up. There are required steps that first-time users don't *really* need to complete right away. And, of course, there are steps that don't *really* need to be there at all. Ring a bell?

Before you develop your straight line, I dare you to sign up for your product and complete all the steps it takes to accomplish a meaningful outcome. As you complete each step, take a screenshot. Even small steps like clicking an "OK" button should make the cut.

If you aren't ready to complete this step yet, here's an example. Let's pretend you're an established ecommerce business with multiple Amazon and eBay stores. Every day you spend three hours manually logging into each account so that you can respond to customer messages. The more eBay and Amazon accounts you have, the more logging in and out of each account you need to do.

After some research, you find that ConnectHero (a company I just made up) has a product that allows you to forward all of your Amazon and eBay messages to a help-desk solution of your choice (e.g. Zendesk).

Once you sign up for ConnectHero's free trial, you're required to integrate your Amazon and eBay accounts with one help-desk solution. Once that's complete, you see messages pop up in your help-desk solution from eBay and Amazon—it's a miracle. This is when you decide that you're going to upgrade once the free trial is over. The product delivered on its promise, and you're a happy camper.

Naturally, ConnectHero wants everyone to get to this point in their user journey, but integrating a help desk with Amazon and eBay isn't easy—users need to take over 50 steps. To make it easier to set up an account, we need to reduce the number of steps. Developing a straight line is the easiest way to do this.

To start, we'll take a screenshot of each step of the onboarding experience. Take screenshots of every step, from the second you land on your homepage until you accomplish a meaningful outcome in the product.

Once you've mapped out all the steps, it's time to label every step.

Label Every Step

Label each step throughout your onboarding experience using the colors green, yellow, or red:

- **Green is absolutely necessary.** Ex. Uploading a piece of JavaScript to your website; asking for an email address to setup an account.

- **Yellow is for advanced features that can be introduced later.** Ex. Setting up a custom signature for your email address; running split tests on your video thumbnails.

- **Red can be removed completely.** Ex. Changing the color of your profile picture; asking for someone's nickname when setting up their account.

Removing your red steps and delaying yellow steps moves you closer to building a highway that speeds users to the promised land.

Develop Your Straight-Line

Growing up in Hamilton, Canada, I took a bus to get to my downtown school. It took between one and two hours. Why the variance? Well, there was no shortage of red and yellow lights in between me and my destination. The bus was constantly starting, stopping, and idling.

To reduce the number of idling cars and speed up traffic, the City of Hamilton introduced a green light sequence for Main Street, the busiest road in the city—and the main road my bus traveled along. If you hit one green light, you kept hitting green lights until you turned off Main Street.

This one innovation helped me get to school 25% faster.

If we go back to our hypothetical example of Amazon and eBay account integration, these might be the first three steps:

1. Integrate your Amazon account.

2. Set up your custom signature.

3. Share your nickname.

Integrating your Amazon account is a must, so we'll label it green. Setting your custom signature is an advanced step. Do you need a custom signature to see incoming messages from Amazon and eBay? Not at all. Once you see the product's value, it'll make sense to complete this step. For now, we'll label this step yellow. Lastly, sharing your nickname is totally unnecessary. Hence, we're going to label this step red and remove it completely.

When it comes to your product, cut out as many red and yellow lights as possible. You'll create shortcuts for your user to experience the desired outcome of your product. If you've already broken down each step between sign-up and the desired outcome, meet with your team to discuss all the steps you can potentially remove. Include people from the product, engineering, marketing, and sales teams if you want a lively discussion.

One of the reasons I love the straight-line system is because there is no bullshit. You will learn that your users simply need to complete steps X, Y, and Z for you to deliver on your product's value.

Even if we create the best-possible experience, we're still going to see lots of users get stuck in the gutters (and never return to our product). Others will go off-track, and we need to plan for detours. We can do that with bumpers that keep users on the straight line to their desired outcome.

The Two Bumpers You Need

As in bowling, we need two bumpers to keep our ball out of the gutter. We can use product and conversational bumpers to guide users to a key outcome.

- **Product bumpers** are mission critical. They help users adopt the product within the application itself.

- **Conversational bumpers** work to educate users, bring them back into the application, and eventually upgrade their account.

To guide users to a desired outcome in the product, you need both bumpers.

Common product bumpers:

- Welcome Messages
- Product Tours
- Progress Bars
- Checklists
- Onboarding Tooltips
- Empty States

Common conversational bumpers:

- User Onboarding Emails
- Push Notifications
- Explainer Videos
- Direct Mail

Conversational Bumpers **Product Bumpers**

Even if you're familiar with these tools, I'll walk through each. You'll be confident that you're using them in a way that will increase your number of customers. Write down the ones you haven't tried yet or need to update. Then, create a list of inputs to run through in your next Triple A sprint.

Product Bumpers

Product bumpers help users experience meaningful

value in the product. Out of the two bumpers, product bumpers are arguably the most important. That's because if you help people accomplish something meaningful in their life with your product, they'll come back on their own.

That's not to say that conversational bumpers aren't useful—they just play a different role. For instance, if someone signs up but never touches foot in your product, the best product bumper in the world won't help you.

Given the importance of product bumpers, I want you to identify one or two that can guide your users to the promised land. Maybe there's an area in your onboarding that could benefit from a progress bar or checklist. Who knows?!

Here are the main product bumpers I'll break down:

1. Welcome Messages;

2. Product Tours;

3. Progress Bars;

4. Checklists;

5. Onboarding Tooltips.

6. Empty States.

1. Welcome Messages

If you knock on a door to a friend's house, what kind

of response would you expect? Would your friend welcome you? Or would they not say a single word, letting you walk around their house and eat the food in the fridge?

The second scenario sounds weird. Friends say hello to friends. But in user onboarding, companies often forget to welcome guests who sign up for a product. It's a "help yourself to the kitchen" mentality. As a user, it can feel odd. We have an innate desire to feel welcomed.

In this example by ConnectHero, they showcase a message from the CEO that personally welcomes the user to the product.

ConnectHero

Welcome, Jennifer!

My name is Matt Brown, founder of ConnectHero, and I'm so glad to see you here! Since we founded the company in 2010, we've been able to help 100's of incredible companies like WeatherTech, Dell, and Nike save countless hours responding to customer messages. Now, I can't wait to help your ecommerce businesses!

Matt Brown
CEO & Founder of ConnectHero

Next →

• • • • • • •

The message explains why the founder created the product and restates the value proposition. Welcome messages can also increase a user's motivation for using the product by clearly explaining the value and building suspense.

Key Takeaways:

1. Welcome messages are your opportunity to greet new users and make them feel invited—you are the host, after all.

2. In addition to saying hello, use them as an opportunity to restate your value proposition and increase users' motivation before they use the product.

3. Welcome messages can also set expectations for what users will experience with your product.

Now that we've welcomed new users, it's time to help them set up their account—fast.

2. Product Tours

Product tours are the ultimate product bumper. They eliminate distractions and give you only a few important options. In my experience, I reserve product tours for the most important green-light items in your straight line. I recommend using only three to five steps in your product tour.

As you can see below, ConnectHero uses a product tour to help us select which help desk solution we'd like to integrate:

ConnectHero

With this approach, your response can trigger a different straight-line onboarding track—one that's specific to *your* desired outcome (e.g. forwarding your Amazon and eBay messages to Zendesk).

If you have a multi-product business, using a product tour at the beginning of your onboarding can be a gamechanger. You catapult people into the areas of the product that they care most about.

If you have a simple consumer application, you might be able to get away without using a product tour. But if you have a complex product with features that accomplish different tasks, a product tour is a must.

I recommend using a "focus mode" that hides background elements to minimize the initial number of choices. Such product tours are extremely effective because they leverage Hick's Law (decision time increases with every additional choice) and the Paradox of Choice (more choices make people less likely to choose).

By eliminating the number of decisions a new user has to make, you increase the likelihood that they will make the right decision. When structuring your product tour, don't reinvent the wheel. Include some of the required green steps in your straight line to help your product deliver on its value faster.

Key Takeaways:

1. Product tours should ask users what they're trying to accomplish in the product.

2. Product tours should cover important step(s) that set users up for success with the product.

3. High-performing product tours often use a "focus mode" that strips away unnecessary elements, like the navigation bar, until the user completes the product tour.

4. Product tours are typically between three and five steps.

All in all, product tours are one of the most effective ways to bump users toward experiencing meaningful value in the product. Typically, this kind of forceful bump is best deployed at the beginning of a user journey; however, as the user progresses along your straight line, you might want to use a more gentle bump, such a progress bars.

3. Progress Bars

Progress bars indicate how far a user has come, and how far they need to go. When running a marathon, I look forward to seeing the markers for each kilometer—they remind me of how far I've run and how far I have to go.

At first, it can be demotivating to see that you've run only 1 out of 42 kilometers. However, once you get close to the 30-kilometer mark, your motivation goes up. You push yourself harder until you cross the finish line.

The same principle holds true for user onboarding. Humans are addicted to progress and will work hard to finish something once they think it's achievable. One caveat: Goals need to seem realistic. Just think of how demoralizing it would be to sign up for an account only to see a progress bar with "0 out of 99" steps completed.

Break down goals to make them achievable. Think about a marathon. Forty-two kilometers sounds intimidating, but dividing it into nine 5-kilometer races helps you feel like you're constantly making progress.

Progress bars can come in many shapes and sizes. According to Formisimo,[39] here are the most common progress bars:

If we were to put what we just learned into action, we could simply add a progress bar to our product tour for ConnectHero. Voila!

ConnectHero

Now, we're setting an expectation for how many steps are ahead for our users. This reassures them that the onboarding process won't take long, and that they're only a few steps from completion. As a result, users are more likely to stick around.

Key Takeaway:

- Effective progress bars start with a substantial percentage of the bar already filled. This helps users feel like they're already underway instead of starting from scratch, and it increases the desire to complete the task.

After initial setup is complete—and progress bars are filled—what's next? You often need to give specific instructions. Onboarding checklists are a great way to go.

4. Onboarding Checklists

Checklists break down big tasks into bite-sized ones. For ConnectHero, we could use an onboarding checklist to help users set up their account:

ConnectHero

Let's Supercharge Zendesk

By installing ConnectHero in Zendesk, you're one step closer to answering all of your marketplace messages in one place.

zendesk ➤ ConnectHero

Install ConnectHero

amazon

- ☑ Select Marketplace
- ☑ Select Amazon
- ☑ Select country
- ○ Connect Amazon
- ○ Test Connection
- ○ Set up Email
- ○ Done

But checklists alone can take you only so far. If you want to get the most out of your onboarding checklists, have them partly filled out by the time the user sees them. This simple tactic employs the "endowed progress effect"[40] —people who think they're close to completing something are more likely to see it through.

As Samuel Hulick reminds us,

> There was a famous experiment conducted at a car wash, involving those "buy X and get one free" loyalty punch cards. They gave half the customers a ten-wash card with two "starter punches" and gave the other half an eight-wash card with no punches, then checked back later on to see at what rate the two groups filled their cards up with punches.
>
> It turned out that the first group got their free wash at almost twice the rate of the second, even though both groups needed the same exact amount of punches to get there. Why? Well, when you have two punches out of ten, you perceive yourself as already being 20% of the way to completion, while the no-punch group was starting out at 0%.

In addition to giving users an overview of how to set up their account, checklists simultaneously increase user motivation because users know how many steps it takes. For best results, I recommend having between three and five checklist items for a new user to complete.

According to Zapier,[41] onboarding checklists also work well because of the Zeigarnik Effect,[42] our tendency to think about incomplete tasks more than completed ones. Not finishing a task nags at us. Researchers call this "task tension." Only completing the task can relieve it.

It's why cliffhangers are effective in movies and television. It's why crossing off an item on your to-do list feels satisfying. It's also why seeing 59 unread Facebook Messages might freak you out.

Key Takeaways:

1. Checklists can motivate new users to complete crucial set-up tasks.

2. Checklists can turn complex, multi-step processes—such as scheduling a month of social media content—into simple, achievable tasks.

3. Onboarding checklists employ the Endowed Progress and Zeigarnik Effect.

If there are specific actions that users need to complete, onboarding is an effective way to motivate users. However, sometimes you also need to *show* users how to do something. That's where onboarding tooltips come in.

5. Onboarding Tooltips

Onboarding tooltips help users learn how to use a product. They can reduce the burden on support and scale usability. Here are the main ways you can use hotspots and action-driven tooltips:

1. Show first-time users how to use the product.

2. Offer helpful tips to new users. Think of this like coaching.

3. Show experienced users new areas of the product they might never have tried otherwise. This is great for increasing retention.

For ConnectHero, we could simply use a tooltip to provide some more context behind what's required for them to setup their account.

Or, we could use a tooltips to show people around important areas of the product. A benefit onboarding tooltips is that they're relatively easy to set up if you use a tool like Appcues, GainsightPX, WalkMe, or Pendo.

However, a lot of companies use onboarding tooltips incorrectly. Tell me if this sounds familiar? You log in to a product for the first time, then a tooltip pops up and tells you to click on a feature. Then, the tooltip prompts you to click on *another* feature. Once clicked, another tooltip offers to show you yet another feature until you've explored the entire product.

This is tooltip abuse. None of the activity leads the user toward experiencing meaningful value in the product. Remember Samuel Hullick's note: "People do not use software simply because they have tons of spare time and find clicking buttons enjoyable."

Key Takeaways:

1. Use onboarding tooltips to guide users toward experiencing meaningful value in the product.

2. People do not use software because they have tons of spare time and love to click buttons.

Onboarding tooltips can be a great way to show people what to do within a product. But what should you show people the first time they see your product's dashboard? Dummy data? That won't get anyone excited about a product. Nor does it help us get closer to experiencing value. If prospects had wanted to see dummy data, they would have signed up for a demo.

Instead of showing dummy data, explore empty states. They can guide users through the first few steps of setting up their account while being less intrusive than a product tour.

6. Empty States

Upon first login, most software applications are boring. There's no data specific to you; it's just the raw application. So what should you show people? An empty state can show people what they need to do to set up their account and experience meaningful value.

For ConnectHero, this could simply be showing people the steps they need to take to complete their account setup.

One of the benefits of empty states is that you immediately show users what needs to be done.

Gmail uses an empty state to help users set up and personalize their account:

Story Chief has an empty state to encourage users to craft their first story:

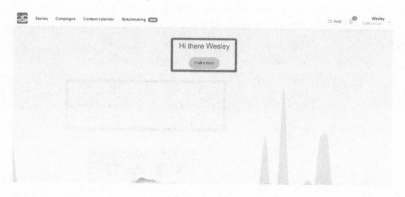

Buffer's empty state encourages you to connect your social media accounts. No one will use Buffer unless they complete this step. As such, Buffer ensures that people connect their social media accounts right away.

To decide what to include in an empty state, ask yourself:

- What steps does a user need to complete to experience a quick win?

- What is the most important step in my straight line?

- How can I make sure that the majority of users complete this step?

Takeaways:

1. Empty states are useful for when a user first lands on a product's dashboard.

2. Empty states should prompt users to take an action that will lead them closer to experiencing meaningful value in the product.

Do you *have* to use empty states, onboarding tooltips, checklists, and product tours? Absolutely not. Use product bumpers only when there's a need. The context in which you use each determines how effective it is.

Now that we've covered the main product bumpers, let's see how conversational bumpers can complement our onboarding.

Conversational Bumpers

Conversational bumpers educate users, bring them back into the application, encourage them to upgrade their account, and notify users of new features. Whether you're using email, push notifications, explainer videos, direct mail, or even SMS, any communication medium can be a bumper.

Here's why you need conversational bumpers in your onboarding:

1. Educate users.

2. Set the right expectations.

3. Meet users where they are and pull them back into your app.

4. Increase motivation to use and buy your product.

One of the best ways to educate users and set the right expectations is through user onboarding emails; however, you can use the same content ideas for push notifications, direct mail, etc.

User Onboarding Emails

The primary function of user onboarding emails is to do something your site can't: go get your users where they are and pull them back into your app. That's to say, if your gym members aren't showing up, user onboarding emails drive out to their house and haul them out of bed on your behalf. That said, the end goal of user onboarding emails is to eventually not need them, in the same way that you don't permanently install training wheels — the point is to help see the adjustment period through, then let the "real" use take over. For software, that means habitual & unprompted use. To accomplish this, user onboarding emails should be set up to nudge people along through the most critical inflection points of the journey from signup to thriving user. They're kind of like a joint between two bones, in that sense: acting as the connective tissue that links one key activity to the next. – *Customer.io*

A main challenge with user onboarding emails is figuring out which emails you need to send. To simplify the process, I've compiled a list of the top nine user onboarding emails:

1. Welcome Emails;

2. Usage Tips;

3. Sales Touches;

4. Usage Reviews;

5. Case Study;

6. Better Life;

7. Post-Trial Survey;

8. Expiry Warning/Trial Extension;

9. Customer Welcome Emails.

The best user onboarding emails are an extension of your product. They have a magical ability to reach beyond your app or site to bring people back and move them toward customer happiness.

To get the most out of each section, draft a version of your user onboarding emails as we go through them. If you need to grab your pencil or laptop, I can wait.

Welcome Email

Welcome emails are triggered as soon as someone signs up for an account. One of the best parts about welcome emails is the high open rate. Aim for at least a 60% open rate.

Given that it's relatively easy to capture people's attention in a welcome email, what content should you put in it? It's tempting to write a lot about the product and ask the user to upgrade. I know you've got numbers to hit, but I encourage you not to take that approach.

Your welcome emails have two purposes. First, you need to train your audience to open your emails. Second, you need to set expectations for what's coming next.

With that in mind, make sure your welcome email has a clear call to action. If you recently launched your product, you can learn a lot by asking, "Why did you sign up to use our product?" Eventually, this will help you pinpoint the desired outcome that people have for your product.

If you're at a loss for words when drafting your welcome emails, don't worry. Here are two examples of welcome emails that follow the recommendations above:

Welcome Email 1

Subject: a personal hello

Body:

Hey,

I'm one of the co-founders of [Your Company], and I'm excited you've decided to sign up.

The [Your Company] Team and I have poured our heart and soul into making [key outcome your product solves for] suck less, so I get really fired up when someone new, like you, joins the ranks.

My top priority is to make sure that you're able to [insert value proposition], so if you have any questions about our product, the website, or even my lackluster mustache, feel free to reply directly to this email.

I hope you can [accomplish key outcome in product]! Stay in touch!

P.S. Yes, I'm a real human.

— Wes, Co-Founder

Welcome Email 2

Subject: you're in — [company name]

Body:

Hey, thanks again for checking out [Your Company]. We help you:

- Customer benefit 1 ("You don't have to worry about X anymore.")

- Customer benefit 2 ("You can finally actually achieve Y, and in less time.")

- Customer benefit 3 ("It's free for the first month.")

But none of that's going to happen if you don't get started.

==> create your first dashboard here <== (your action-worded CTA)

Talk soon,

Wes

Key Takeaways:

- Welcome emails have the highest open rates of all user onboarding emails.

- Your welcome emails should train your audience to open your emails and set expectations for what's coming next.

- To make sure your audience receives this email (and that it doesn't get caught in a lovely spam filter), I recommend using plain text and no images, at least for the first email.

Welcome emails shouldn't be complicated. At some point, however, you have to get a bit more technical and offer a helping hand. That's when usage-tip emails come in handy.

Usage-Tip Emails

Usage-tip emails are helpful nudges that direct users to take steps in the product that set them up for success.

Be careful about what you encourage. For instance, if an activity you're encouraging doesn't help them experience meaningful value in the product, you dampen user motivation. Don't send emails that ask users to complete items that aren't part of your straight-line onboarding track.

In general, usage-tip emails should do three things:

1. Direct users to a specific product page (e.g. "Manage Users" page).

2. Link to specific help-center articles or blog posts (e.g. "How to invite a user from outside your company").

3. Give actionable best practices or invite abandoned users to return.

If you can do these three things, you'll help more users succeed. Wistia's Soapbox product is a perfect example. After I created my first video, they sent a usage-tip email to encourage me to share it with someone.

This email helped me learn more about Wistia's features but also made it easier to experience meaningful value by sharing the video.

Key Takeaways:

1. Usage-tip emails nudge users to take steps in the product that set them up for success.

2. The best usage tips are trigger-based and sent out once you do or don't complete an onboarding task.

If users miss a step in their straight-line onboarding track, usage-tip emails can bump them toward the next step without being intrusive. Nevertheless, you'll eventually need to ask for the sale.

Sales-Touch Emails

Sales-touch emails are exactly what the name implies. These emails can be automated, but the most important part is timing. If you send your sales-touch emails too soon, you'll turn people away. If you send them too late, you'll miss out on sales. The sweet spot for sending sales-touch emails is as soon as you deliver on your value, according to the UCD Model we covered in Part II.

For Databox, this is when you create and customize your first dashboard.

Sales Touch Email 1

Subject: The hard part is over...

Body:

Hi Wesley,

You already did all the work to customize Databox and the hard part is over...

Were you left with any questions? If so, let me know and I will answer them. Here are some common questions I get:

- How to visualise goals and events from Google Analytics

- Can I build dashboard with data stored in Google Sheets

- Is it possible to push custom data via API

- Do you offer a partner program for agencies

Would love to learn more about you and what are you looking to accomplish with Databox. Just hit "reply" and let me know.

Thanks,

Andrew

Notice how the email doesn't come across as "salesy." The goal of the message is to help me get more value out of the platform. For your sales-touch emails, try two things:

1. Frame your sales-touch emails as a "success meeting" to celebrate the user achieving their desired outcome and to show them how to get more out of the product.

2. Invite inactive users to an orientation demo (e.g. "30-minute crash course on how to share documents and collaborate between teams").

You'll find that these "sales" emails are generally well received. Users will be happy to hear what you have to say.

If you're looking for a great template, Claire Suellentrop from Userlist.io shared a great email you can use:

Sales Touch Email 2

Subject: [Intriguing phrase about how a paid feature will make their lives easier.]

Hi {{user.first_name | default: "there"}},

[Pain point referenced in subject line] is no fun. [Describe a few problems the pain point causes, e.g. keeps them at the office late in the evening, forces them to delete important files or scatter them across multiple locations, wastes precious hours each week preparing for meetings and then having to reschedule.]

With [paid feature], you'll [get huge benefit, e.g. have the freedom to take Friday afternoons off, rest easy knowing their files are all in one place, increase productivity by 18%].

Since [paid feature] is part of our [paid plan name] plan, you'll just want to upgrade to [paid plan name] and you'll be good to go!

Just head to your billing page now, so you can start [getting benefit] [link].

Talk soon,
[Signature]

Takeaways:

- The sweet spot for sending sales-touch emails is as soon as someone experiences meaningful value in your product.

- Craft sales-touch emails to help users get more value out of the platform.

As you can see, sales-touch emails are largely about timing and offering a helpful hand. However, sometimes we still need to clarify our product's value to build a convincing case to upgrade. One of the best ways to do that is through case-study emails.

Case-Study Emails

As Joanna Wiebe from Copyhackers[43] notes, case studies are great—as long as you tell the story right. And by "tell the story right," I mean be a good storyteller:

- Open with a hook.

- Lure the reader from one line to the next.

- Start in the middle of the action.

- Create compelling characters.

- Set the story around a central conflict.

If you don't have conflict, you don't have a story (or a hook). And who would read that?

Whether you send a case-study email that includes a video testimonial,[44] customer story, or old-fashioned case study, tell your customer's story about using the product. Invision does this by showcasing some of the incredible designs their customers have created with the product.

Meet some other genius designers who use InVision

You're in good company

Tons of talented designers use InVision every day. Here's your chance to meet them.

Every Inside Design gives you a sneak peek at how design works at amazing companies. Discover how other designers work, get inspired, and build the amazing tools we use every day.

TAKE A SNEAK PEEK

🐦 TWEET   f SHARE   g⁺ SHARE

DESIGN BETTER EXPERIENCES FOR WEB & MOBILE
A Prototyping, Collaboration & Workflow Platform

GET STARTED • FREE FOREVER!

InVision App   41 Madison Ave   Floor 25   New York, NY   10010   USA

Thanks for being part of the InVision Design Community! I've sent this to you as part of our Marketing Information series.

Unsubscribe

How do you decide which testimonials to showcase? One of the best ways to decide is based on the objections you regularly receive when selling your product. These objections could be:

- The price is too high.

- We don't have the budget.

- It's not important right now.

Pair your top objection with a testimonial that addresses the objection head on. For instance, if your top objection is that the price is too high, include a testimonial that showcases the amount of value the customer received from using your product. You address a top objection head on, with your testimonial doing the heavy lifting.

If you send case-study emails before selling users on your product, you'll improve your free-to-paid conversion rate.[45]

Key Takeaways:

- Use case-study emails to combat objections that users might have before they enter the buying phase.

- Make sure that each case-study email answers "What's in it for me?" for users.

Case studies are a powerful way to combat objections. However, sometimes we still need to communicate product benefits. One of the best ways to do this is through better-life emails.

Better-Life Emails

Better-life emails communicate the benefits of the product. The main call to action in these emails is often to upgrade an account. But you can also direct people to try specific features.

Better-life emails don't tell a customer story. They focus on communicating the benefits of the product. Twist uses better-life emails to encourage people to "take back the workday" and sign up their team.

twist

Launch Twist

Take back the workday

According to the Harvard Business Review, knowledge workers spend as much as **80% of the workday** just communicating – in meetings, on calls, via email and group chat.

Changing the way you collaborate is hard. But imagine what you could accomplish if you gave your team the tools to focus on doing their best work instead of constantly responding to emails and group chats.

If you're not sure if Twist is a good fit for your team – or if you need help convincing your coworkers to get onboard – here's a short article to help you make the right decision:

How Twist can help your team →

Ready to start now? Invite your team

Our best,
The Twist team

"Now that we're using Twist we spend less time digging through overflowing inboxes and searching through outdated chat conversations."

 —Ellen Luccock
Director of Client Relations, The Management Coach

What Twist users have to say...   See all quotes →

Stay in touch with your team from anywhere. Download the apps

Blog | Twitter | Help Center

Unsubscribe from Twist tips

Image credit: Reallygoodemails.com

Showcase how your product improves a user's life. If you're selling a business intelligence tool, highlight how the user will no longer need to spend countless hours crunching numbers in Excel.

A common mistake with better-life emails is focusing only on the functional outcome of your product. Remember: You need to account for functional, social, and emotional outcomes. Here's a breakdown of each:

- **Functional outcome.** The core tasks that customers want to get done.

- **Emotional outcome.** How customers want to feel, or avoid feeling, as a result of the functional task.

- **Social outcome.** How customers want to be perceived by others.

If you know the three reasons why people buy your product, you can boost your conversion rate and ultimately acquire more customers. Before writing your better-life emails, ask yourself these questions:

- When talking to potential buyers, what benefits get them most excited?

- What benefits make it a no-brainer for people to upgrade?

You'll have a better idea of which benefits to feature.

Key Takeaways:

- Better-life emails showcase the benefits of your product.

- The call to action can ask users to upgrade or help users experience product benefits for themselves.

Product-led companies often forget to emphasize the better life that their product offers during the trial period. By assuming users know the benefits, you miss an opportunity to restate your value and build a convincing case. If you have a free trial, that's a critical window: You have limited time to do so.

Expiry-Warning Emails

Expiry-warning emails remind the user to upgrade before a free trial ends. Freemium models don't use expiry-warning emails because part of the product is free forever. That said, if you have a hybrid model (with a free trial and freemium offer), expiry emails can still motivate users to upgrade.

If you have an opt-out free trial[46] (you require a credit card upfront), you *must* send expiry-warning emails. If you don't, you're guaranteed to annoy users and flood your support reps with refund demands. Think about it: What did you do the last time you signed up for a product with a credit card and missed the deadline?

Did you continue paying for the product for a month or two before realizing you forgot to cancel? Or did you demand support give you a refund because you forgot to cancel your plan?

I won't dive into whether you should or shouldn't have a credit-card requirement during the free-trial sign-up, but, as a general rule, make it easy for users to cancel their account. Squarespace sends emails to notify users that their trial will expire soon. This email is great because it restates the value proposition and why it makes sense to upgrade now.

Your free trial expires in 24 hours.

Your 14-day trial for http://amy-smith-podj.squarespace.com ends in 24 hours and we hope you've enjoyed the experience. Our plans start at $8 per month and by upgrading now, you'll ensure your website stays live and can take full advantage of these great features:

CLOUD HOSTING	SITE ANALYTICS	FREE DOMAIN	24/7 SUPPORT

Have questions about upgrading?

Our support team can answer any question about upgrading to a full Squarespace account. We're on call 24 hours a day, 7 days a week, and respond to all questions in under an hour. If you need assistance, contact us anytime by visiting our Help Center.

Let us know if there's anything we can do.

According to PostMark App,[47] expiry-warning emails have three goals:

1. Set clear expectations.

Trials end—that's just how they work. However, if users provide a credit card as part of the sign-up process, they'll be charged automatically. Make sure to give them a few days notice about the charge so they aren't surprised.

The last thing you want to do is annoy users who forgot that they signed up for your product and paid accidentally. When they figure out that they were charged, they'll demand a refund.

Even if you don't require a credit card, you want to craft a painless transition to paying customer.

The best way to do that is by:

- Giving users as much notice as possible.

- Making it crystal clear when the trial expires and what happens if the trial expires.

- Providing a call to action for users to upgrade.

2. Make it easy for users to upgrade, cancel, or do nothing.

Some people will upgrade, and some won't. As such, you want it to be easy for people to upgrade. Still, most people won't upgrade, so it should be easy for users to cancel their account. The expiry email can make this process easy and leave a positive impression.

3. Communicate how users can get help.

The transition from trial to paying customer can be stressful. Once a customer decides to use your software, they want to make the transition seamless. When will they be charged? How can they get approval from their team? In some cases, they may also wonder if they can maintain data from their current trial.

There are countless questions and concerns. Make sure that customers know that they can get help and know where to find it. Even if you check the box on all of the recommended ways of using expiry emails, you need to avoid some common mistakes.

Common mistakes with expiry-warning emails

Trial expiration emails serve two very different user types:

1. People who want to become paying customers;

2. People who don't.

In the same email, you need to address the needs of *both* groups—without making the email confusing. Most mistakes in expiry-warning emails stem from these conflicting goals.

1. Failing to provide enough advanced notice

Weekends, vacations, and travel can interfere with the timing of a trial expiration. It's important to give people a heads up. That way, users know exactly when a trial will expire, whether they want to transition to paying customer (and avoid a service interruption), or if they want to cancel their account (and avoid an unintentional payment).

I recommend sending an expiry-warning email at least three days before the end of each user's trial. This gives users enough time to make a decision to move forward with your product or not.

2. *Assuming that the recipient wants to begin paying for the product*

One of the biggest mistakes I see companies make with expiry-warning emails is not including the product's main value proposition. Offering a compelling reason to take action results in (surprise) more people taking action.

Just because someone signs up for a free trial doesn't mean that they're ready to buy. Most people who sign up for your free trial or freemium model won't convert. You need to include compelling reasons for someone to upgrade. Screenhero proves this point by failing to include a convincing reason to upgrade.

⟨⟩ Screenhero

Hi Matthew,

Thanks for signing up for Screenhero. We hope you have been enjoying your free trial.

Unfortunately, your free trial is ending in 3 days.

We'd love to keep you as a customer, and there is still time to complete your subscription! Simply visit your account dashboard to subscribe.

As a reminder, when your trial expires you will be automatically placed on the free guest plan.

If you have any questions or feedback, just reply to this email, and we'll get right back to you.

-- The Screenhero Team

On the other hand, Squarespace's expiry email does a great job highlighting the key benefits of the platform. Now we know why we should upgrade, right?

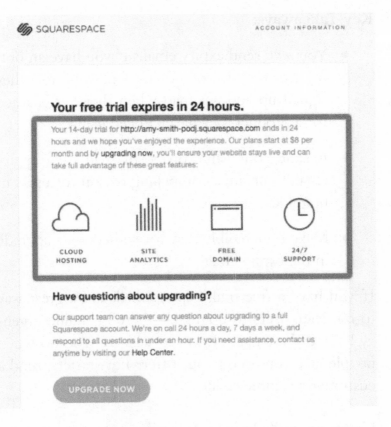

To recap, your expiry-warning emails should be able to answer these questions:

1. Why should I upgrade?

2. How do I upgrade?

3. How much time do I have left?

4. What happens when the trial is over?

5. How do I cancel? (if you require a credit card)

6. Where can I go if I need help?

Key Takeaways:

- You *must* send expiry emails if you have an opt-out free trial. If you don't, users will forget they signed up and get mad when they get charged for a product they haven't been using.

- Restate your value proposition in each expiry email to create a compelling reason for users to upgrade.

- Make it incredibly easy for someone to upgrade in the expiry email.

If you have a free trial, expiry emails are a great way to motivate users to upgrade—there's genuine urgency behind the email. However, what do you do when people take you up on your offer? For starters, send a customer-welcome email.

Customer-Welcome Emails

Have you ever purchased a plane ticket on a questionable travel website, then waited nervously for email confirmation? When you buy something from a brand you don't trust, waiting for a confirmation email can feel like an eternity. Your new customers feel the same way.

To reduce that anxiety, use customer-welcome emails:

1. Reassure users that they made the right decision.

2. Remind users of what they can do with the platform.

3. Set expectations for what comes next (e.g. Will a customer success rep reach out?).

Too many businesses don't welcome new customers immediately. Most reach out manually, but it takes time. In the interim, new customers become nervous, wondering if they made the right decision. Don't make your new customer think twice. Remind them why they made the right decision. Spotify welcomes users as soon as they upgrade to premium:

Image credit to reallygoodemails.com

One thing Spotify has done really well is to remind users *why* they upgraded, showcasing the value of the platform. This email increases user motivation to check out the product and listen to some great music without ads. If you have a freemium product, recap your premium features so that users can explore them right away.

Key Takeaways:

- Customer-welcome emails must be sent as soon as users upgrade.

- The point of customer-welcome emails is to reassure users that they made the right decision, remind them what they can now do with the platform, and set expectations for what comes next.

Customer-welcome emails are a great way to remind new customers that they made the right choice. But no matter how hard you try, not everyone will convert— nor should they. Your product might not be the right fit. It might be too expensive. The list goes on.

To improve your free-trial experience, you need to learn why it didn't work out for some users.

This is why I almost always recommend using post-trial survey emails.

Post-Trial Survey Emails

Even with the most amazing free-trial experience, most users won't convert. Some aren't a good fit. Some might have not have had time to check out your tool. Others, well, they might have needed more time or someone to help them learn to use the product.

There are countless reasons, but you'll never learn understand them if you don't implement post-trial survey emails. For Autopilot, there post-trial survey email looks like this:

Post-Trial Survey Email 1

Subject: Wesley, have 60 seconds to share why?

Body:

Hi Wesley,

I noticed that you have not purchased Autopilot so far. I'd love to hear your thoughts on your trial experience in this super quick survey. It will only take 60 seconds (we have measured it!)

Your response will help us focus on improving your trial experience and better meet your needs.

Thanks in advance,

Lauren

What I like about this email is how it gets straight to the point and encourages you to fill out a quick survey:

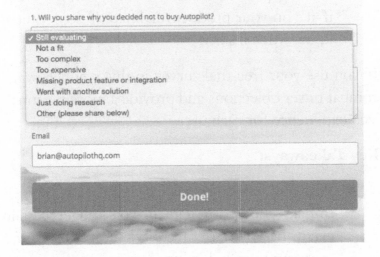

Based on your response, Autopilot[48] enrolls you in an automated sequence. Autopilot recommends starting with this list:

- Still evaluating → Offer a trial extension

- Not a fit → Drop into nurture

- Too complex → Schedule a customer success call

- Too expensive → Provide a one-time discount

- Went with another solution → Send top-of-funnel lead-nurturing emails to stay top-of-mind if the other service doesn't work out

- Just doing research → Add to nurture (notice the nurturing trend?)

- Missing product feature or integration → See if it's on your product roadmap; if so, let them know when it's live

If you use your free-trial survey in this manner, you'll combat buyer objections and provide a more personalized experience for each user.

Key Takeaways:

- Post-trial survey emails can improve your free-to-paid conversion rate if you trigger certain events based on user feedback. For instance, if a user says the product was too complex, you can have a customer success representative reach out to walk them through the product.

As in bowling, if you don't get a strike in the first throw, you have another shot. So, why not use post-trial survey emails as a way to rekindle the opportunity and provide an incredible experience? After all, these same users were interested in using your product for a specific reason. Let's help them out.

Now that we've gone through all of the user onboarding emails, let's do a quick review.

User Onboarding Emails Overview

Even with the best copy in the world, if your onboarding experience lacks personalization, you'll lose out on conversions. Imagine that I just signed up for your product and spent several hours using it during the first couple of days. I've gone through all of your onboarding tooltips and experienced the value of your product numerous times. I'm a power user and am sold on your product. I love it!

Now, imagine what must be going through my head when you send me an email on how to complete a very basic step in your onboarding process—one that I've already completed. I'll look at this email for two seconds and make several assumptions:

1. You have no idea that I've already done this action item three times.

2. This is one-size-fits-all onboarding.

3. Your emails are pointless.

I still love your product, but compare that to another potential experience. Imagine, three days into my trial, you notice that I'm getting incredible value out of the platform. You send me a timely email asking if I want to upgrade. Since I'm already sold on your product, I convert on day four of your free trial.

There's a big difference between these two scenarios. The first experience wasn't relevant, while the second recognized where I was in the user journey.

For most free trials, here's what a user onboarding email sequence looks like:

1. Day 1: Welcome email;

2. Day 3: Content to educate user;

3. Day 5: Check-in demo;

4. Day 8: Product features;

5. Day 12: Expiry-warning email.

This is a one-size-fits-all approach. It doesn't serve any of the outliers below:

- If you're a power user and keep receiving product-feature emails for a feature you've already used, they're pointless.

- If you've never logged into the product, why should you receive advanced lessons on how to use it?

- If you already upgraded and continue to receive these emails, how does that feel?

The only way to avoid these scenarios and improve your free-to-paid conversion rate is to create a smart conversational bumper system.

Create a Smart Conversational Bumper System

Smart signals tell us when we should send a specific conversational bumper to keep users on a straight line. Here are the four main signals:

1. Signup;

2. Quick win;

3. Desired outcome;

4. Customer.

Each signal tells us about where the user is in their journey. Based on the signal, we can enroll people into different email onboarding tracks. For instance, if someone experiences a quick win in the product, we can send emails on how to dive deeper into the product. Or, if someone experiences a desired outcome, we can send sales-touch and case-study emails to encourage users to upgrade.

For the onboarding tracks below, I want to point out one detail that's easy to miss. If you see a lightning bolt underneath the email, it's a trigger-based email. If you see a clock underneath an email, it's time-based. Now, that we're on the same page, let's dive in!

Conversational Bumper Track 1: Quick Win

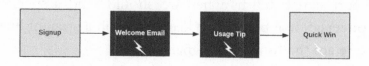

- **Signal**: Signup

- **Key Outcome**: Quick Win

As you can see above, when someone signs up, it signals the start of the conversational bumper track. A sign-up should trigger a welcome email immediately. Depending on how complex your product is, you might need one or even five usage-tip emails to support account setup.

As we covered earlier, usage-tip emails do three things:

1. Direct users to a specific product page (e.g. "Manage Users" page).

2. Link to help-center articles or blog posts (e.g. "How to invite a user from outside your company").

3. Give actionable best practices or invite back abandoned users.

In the first onboarding track, the only thing we care about is getting someone to experience a quick win in the product. If we operate a business intelligence software solution, our first quick win might be setting up a dashboard to visualize our analytics. At first, every email we send to new users should focus on that outcome.

You *don't* need to send usage-tip emails to users if they accomplish the quick win the first time they use your product. Remember, product bumpers also guide users toward achieving their desired outcome. Conversational bumpers are there only if users don't take the required actions we've set out in our straight line.

Let's say you're CrazyEgg, a heat-mapping tool, and your first quick win is getting users to upload a tracking script to their website. If they accomplish this in the first-run onboarding experience, why send more emails about how to upload the script? On the flip side, if you *didn't* upload the script, it would be extremely helpful to send an email that guided users on the process.

Key Takeaways:

- Focus on helping users experience a quick win in the product.

- The only two emails you need to include are welcome and usage-tip emails.

- There's no focus on selling. It's about setting up users for success.

Once your users have accomplished a quick win, it's time to think about how you can turn your new users into repeat users. One of the best ways to do that is to help users achieve their desired outcome in the product.

Conversational Bumper Track 2: Desired Outcome

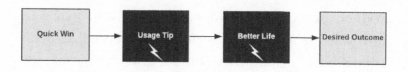

- **Signal**: Quick Win

- **Key Outcome**: Desired Outcome

Conversational Bumper Track 2 starts as soon as someone gets a quick win and ends when someone experiences a desired outcome in your product. Once again, we'll use usage-tip emails; however, we'll focus on helping users experience a desired outcome.

Do you really need Track 2? It really depends on your product. If you have a simple product like Netflix, sending usage-tip emails on how to click "Play" is overkill. On the flip side, if you have a complex product, your quick win might have been uploading a piece of JavaScript. Track 2 can drive users closer to their desired outcome.

One reason I've included better-life emails in this mix is because you need to remind users why they signed up. Given that these emails showcase the desired outcome, you want to challenge users to give the product a shot.

Key Takeaway:

- Conversational Bumper Track 2 guides users toward experiencing your product's desired outcome.

Once users have experienced your product's desired outcome, it's time to convert them into customers—if they're a good fit.

Conversational Bumper Track 3: Convert

As Derek Gleason of CXL wrote, "Freemium and free-trial signups have one thing in common: Neither generates revenue." For the first two onboarding tracks, we've avoided revenue generation. That wasn't by accident.

You see, most people go wrong with their conversational bumpers by trying to monetize users too quickly. Skipping the first two bumper tracks, as the English would say, "is a bit forward." If that's you, go back and implement the first two conversational bumper tracks. Without that solid foundation, the strategies and tactics in Track 3 won't be nearly as effective.

At first glance, Conversational Bumper Track 3 looks a bit overwhelming. You have a bunch of different email types:

1. Sales-touch emails;

2. Case-study emails;

3. Trial-expiry emails;

4. Trial-extension emails;

5. Post-trial surveys;

6. Customer-welcome emails.

One of the best parts about Track 3 is that each email focuses on upgrading the user to become a paying customer. You might be thinking, "Wes, if I sent out every email you recommend, I'll overwhelm my users." Not necessarily. Each bumper track is trigger-based. So, if your user experiences a quick win in the product during the first visit, you won't send any usage-tip emails, and you'd auto-enroll them in Conversational Bumper Track 2.

On the other hand, if your user experienced the desired outcome in the first-run onboarding experience but never came back, you'd enroll them in Track 3 to bring them back and upgrade.

The true beauty of the Conversational Bumper Track is that you meet your users where they are in their journey. As soon as a user upgrades, you automatically stop sending them upgrade emails. (Or, at least, I hope you would.)

For Track 3, *how* you reach out to each user depends on the average LTV of each customer. If you have a relatively high LTV, you can afford a higher CAC, so you may want to explore a low-touch sales model as soon as someone experiences the desired outcome. Just remember: You have to match your sales approach with your average LTV. Otherwise, unsustainable CACs will destroy your margins.

Key Takeaways:

- The focus is to upgrade users into customers.

- How you reach out depends on your average LTV. If you don't match your outreach approach with your LTV, you risk running an unprofitable business.

- Once a user upgrades, remove them from Track 3 and send them a customer-welcome email.

Now that we've gone through the three main tracks, it's time to review everything.

Conversational Bumper Review

Your conversational bumpers keep people from going in the gutter and never returning to your product. Conversational bumpers work because they reach people where they are. Whether you decide to use email, SMS, remarketing ads, or direct mail, there are countless ways to bring people back to the product after they leave.

At the end of the day, recall that conversational bumpers are like training wheels on a bike. They're invaluable when you're first learning, but the long-term goal is to make them unnecessary. If you have a great product, people will naturally come back and continue using it. Just think about how many times you check social media in a week. You're hooked.

By now, I hope you see how the bowling alley framework can help you drive more users to become customers without resorting to salesy messaging, discounting, or those "fun" countdown timers. Delivering on the value that you promised builds trust quickly and helps people understand how your solution can help them.

Once a user signs up as a customer, don't think you're off the hook. You still have two more levers to pull to grow your business. First, we're going to cover how to increase your ARPU. Then, we'll dive deep on retention.

CHAPTER 14

Increase Your Average Revenue Per User (ARPU)

A high ARPU means you can scale faster, use more expensive acquisition channels, and ultimately maximize your customer lifetime value. This is not to be confused with nickle-and-diming every customer who comes your way! As Joel Yok puts it:

> On average, a repeat customer will spend 67% more[49] than a new customer. You don't have to be a financial whiz to figure out that an easy, profitable way to grow your business is to sell to existing customers.

In a business world dominated by customer acquisition, ARPU goes against the grain by focusing on capital-efficient growth. It focuses on the quality rather than quantity of customers.

While a high ARPU can show that you're monetizing your user base effectively, however, it's not a perfect metric. One flaw? There's a lot of confusion as to what a "user" is.

How to Define a User

There's no clear-cut definition of a user. It depends on your business. Let's say you run Netflix or Spotify. You'd define a user as someone who's paying you. But in B2B, the word "account" can be synonymous with user, even though an account might have multiple users. Or, if you have a freemium model, only *paying* users would qualify as "users" when calculating ARPU.

These varying definitions can cause confusion. To combat it, teams like ProfitWell use the term Average Revenue Per Paying User (ARPPU) to signal that a user has paid within their billing system. It doesn't matter whether you use ARPU, ARPPU, ARPS, ARPA, or ARPC as your naming convention—as long as everyone within your company is clear on how you calculate it.

Which brings us to...

How Do You Calculate ARPU?

ARPU is one of the easiest metrics you can calculate (once you know how to define a "user").

For SaaS businesses, here's the most common way to calculate ARPU:

ARPU = Total MRR / Total Users

So, imagine this is your business:

- You have $100,000 MRR.

- Right now, you have 5,000 customers.

- Your ARPU is $100,000 / 5,000 = $20.

Now, go on, find out what your ARPU is. Next, we'll put that number to good use.

Why Should You Care about ARPU?

Once you know your ARPU, you'll better understand:

- How to market your business;

- If direct sales makes sense;

- Who your most profitable customers are.

For instance, if your ARPU is only $20, like in the example above, spending $2,000 to acquire a new customer through an enterprise sales effort would take over eight years to break even. If your churn is high, this channel will be a waste of money.

Knowing your ARPU will show you which channels you can afford to use. According to Brian Balfour,[50] CEO at Reforge, if you have a low ARPU, you might want to consider SEO; paid marketing channels might be too expensive. Or, if you have an extremely high ARPU, you can consider hiring an enterprise sales team.

There are no hard rules. But here are some channels to consider based on your ARPU:

High ARPU	Enterprise Sales
Mid ARPU	Inside Sales, Paid Advertising
Low ARPU	SEO, Content Marketing, Virality

Knowing your ARPU will also help you figure out which customers are a good fit. **Not all customers are created equal.** Every time you take a bite of revenue, some tastes great, but a good chunk can be harmful. You don't eat the core of an apple, and you need to train your business not to bite into bad revenue.

Companies with a "grow at all costs" mentality die hard. In the pursuit of rapid growth, they subsist on a revenue diet of mostly junk food. To hit their numbers, teams take on small, distracting, and expensive low-revenue customers.

Don't weigh yourself down with bad revenue. Gorge yourself on customers who are an incredible fit for your business. Let your competitors munch on the bad-fit customers. That will lead to healthier metrics throughout your business, including ARPU.

How Do You Optimize for ARPU?

Below are some of the best strategies and tactics to improve your ARPU.

Use Value Metrics

Whether you're trying to reduce churn, acquire more customers, or optimize for ARPU, using value metrics in your pricing model will help your business grow. Like I mentioned before, product-led businesses marry your revenue with your customer acquisition model. For the marriage to work, both sides need to cooperate.

When it comes to pricing, if you 100x your prices, your customer acquisition model will take a brutal hit. On the other side of the spectrum, if you give away the majority of your features for free, you'll create a powerful customer acquisition model that will bankrupt your business.

Neither option is ideal. You need to find a happy middle ground where both parties can agree on an acceptable level of compromise.

Improve Your Pricing Tiers

Removing unneeded pricing tiers can often increase your ARPU—without raising prices. How? It comes down to the Paradox of Choice,[51] a term coined by Barry Schwartz. It boils down to this: **The more choices you have, the less likely you are to choose.**

This sounds counterintuitive. Many of us—myself included, at one point—assume that more choice means better options and greater satisfaction. But adding more choices unknowingly adds more stress and anxiety to a decision. What happens then? Analysis paralysis. The easiest decision is maintaining the status quo.

To combat this, many SaaS businesses limit pricing options to three or fewer and highlight the most popular plan. By doing so, companies like Teamwork.com have increased ARPU by 20%.[52]

Raise Your Prices

Robert Smith,[53] founder of Vista Equity Partners, believes that most entrepreneurs undervalue the elasticity of demand—which results in them undercharging for their products. Simply increasing your prices for inflation can have an incredible impact on ARPU over the years.

Treat Your Best Users Like the Queen

If the Queen of England came into your home, would you treat her differently than one of your friends who came to "hang out"? You bet. Now, if a perfect-fit user came into your product, would you treat them differently? I hope you would, but it's probably not the case.

According to Liam Boogar-Azoulay, Head of Marketing at MadKudu, optimizing conversions for all users is a fool's errand. When designing experiments to improve onboarding, we forget to ask whether the experiment will help our *best* leads become successful users.

Businesses create operational friction when they introduce hurdles that require their best users to prove they're worthy of a good experience. They expect the best enterprise leads to fill out lengthy forms to self-qualify so that sales reps don't waste time talking to bad leads. They provide great leads with the same generic onboarding experience instead of building one that speaks to their specific motivations.

With an ideal buyer journey, you can generate 80% of your revenue by focusing on 20% of your best leads.

Upselling and Cross-selling

This is the no-brainer strategy to improve your ARPU. Upselling encompasses the sale of additional features, product add-ons, and services. Cross-selling refers to completely different products or services.

HubSpot started with a marketing automation platform but have since built a sales CRM and help-desk solution. These completely new products have helped HubSpot cross-sell to existing customers in a powerful way.

For upselling, if you use value metrics in your pricing model, you'll naturally be able to charge more as customers grow and get more value out of your product. However, you can also upsell via add-ons and services that help customers kick ass at whatever you help them do.

Putting It All Together

Improving your ARPU starts by taking on the right

customers, then growing with them. Not all customers are created equal. Learn whom to ignore.

One of the easiest ways to increase your ARPU is to solve for churn. If you can lock down your churn, you'll grow your business exponentially—increasing the number of good-fit, high-value customers.

CHAPTER 15

Slay Your Churn Beast

Churn is the silent killer of your company. If you don't tackle churn early, you'll be working extremely hard just to stand still.

– Patrick Campbell Co-Founder & CEO, ProfitWell

Churn. It's the arch nemesis of any SaaS business. You'll never kill your churn beast, but you can starve it of the environment it needs to grow. Otherwise, a few bad-fit customers or a terrible onboarding experience can grow your creature into an unforgiving monster.

Everyone knows the risk of churn, and yet so few companies prioritize reducing it. Why? One of the big reasons, according to Buffer's Roy Olende,[54] is that, "Much like it's more exciting to buy a new car than to maintain a current vehicle, it's a lot easier to celebrate new customers than retain customers."

This is crazy, especially when you consider that increasing your customer retention rate by as little as 5% can increase your profits by 25–95%.[55] This is why a shift from an acquisition-first[56] mindset to a retention-first[57] mindset can have an incredible impact on growth.

Since there are countless ways to define churn. Let's make sure we're on the same page.

What Is Churn?

According to HubSpot, customer churn is the percentage of your customers or subscribers who cancel or don't renew their SaaS subscription during a given time period. Here's a hypothetical situation:

- You have 100 customers at the start of the year.

- 10 of them cancel by year's end.

- Your churn rate is $10/100 = 0.10$, or **10% customer churn**.

Most stop here and assume that churn is the same thing as the percentage of customers canceling in a given time period. But not all churn is equal. For instance, you could have a churn rate of less than 1% but see your MRR drop by 40% if your biggest customer leaves.

A holistic approach measures churn in three ways:

1. **Customer Churn.** The number of customers lost in a given time period.

2. **Revenue Churn.** The amount of revenue lost in a given time period.

3. **Activity Churn.** The number of users at risk of churning due to red-flag activity (e.g. not logging into the your application for two months).

Measuring your customer and revenue churn will give you solid monthly metrics. Activity churn will help monitor potential churn before it takes a meaty chunk of your bottom line.

So How Do You Calculate Churn?

According to ProfitWell, there are more than 43 ways to calculate churn. As a result, many companies pick the churn rate or number that looks the prettiest.

As Steli Efti, CEO of Close.io, says, "Don't approach churn by trying to put lipstick on a pig. Churn is one of the most serious, persistent problems that startups face, and the only way to deal with it is through brutal honesty." Put away your lipstick. Let's dive in.

Customer Churn

Customer churn is the easiest and most widely used way to measure churn. All you need to do is divide the number of customers who churned by the total number of customers in a given time period. Multiply that number by 100 to get a percentage:

Customer Churn = (Churned Customers/ Total Customers) x 100

According to Brianne Kimmel,[58] a top angel investor, your customer churn percentage will vary significantly depending on your target audience, which makes perfect sense. Enterprise clients will churn less often— these are established businesses that are resistant to change. SMB clients include many new and emerging companies that often go out of business.

Based on Kimmel's research,[59] here are some of the average churn rates you can expect, depending on your target audience:

Audience	Monthly Customer Churn %	Annual Customer Churn %
SMB	3–7%	31–58%
Mid-Market	1–2%	11–22%
Enterprise	0.5–1%	6–10%

These industry standards are great for a quick look at how you stack up against the market. But at the end of the day, I want you to compete with your own customer churn rate and not use these industry standards as your guide posts. Why? Because it really doesn't matter what the other guy is doing. As you take on your own churn beast, your business will reap the benefits—no matter where you start.

Kristen DeCosta, Growth Marketer at Churn Buster, sees this all the time. Having helped thousands of companies improve their churn rate, she's seen how focusing on industry standards creates confusion, chaos, and stress. It's like creating a lofty sales goal without developing a strategy behind it.

Instead, focus on incremental improvements to your churn rate. This mindset allows you to analyze your situation, find the lowest hanging fruit for your business, and clarify the strategy behind it. Define success against your past self. There is no silver bullet to take down your churn beast. Any improvement is a win. Take it one step at a time and set meaningful internal goals.

Now, let's dig into revenue churn, as it can tell a very different story.

Revenue Churn

Imagine losing your biggest customer next month. Your customer churn rate might look incredible, but your revenue just took a massive hit. That's why understanding your customer churn is a great starting point, but correlating it with your revenue churn offers a much clearer picture.

Here's the formula to calculate your revenue churn:

Revenue Churn = (Churned MRR/Total MRR) x 100

Here's a hypothetical situation:

- You have 1% customer churn and 100 customers.

- However, the one customer you lost accounted for $40,000 MRR.

- If your total MRR was $100,000, your revenue churn is $40,000/100,000 = 0.4$, or 40%.

Your customer churn rate looks great, but your business is bleeding money. Not all churn has a clear before-and-after. Churn can happen weeks, months, or even years before someone pulls the plug. This is known as activity churn.

Activity Churn

As Des Traynor[60] notes,

> Typically customers gradually stop using products, from using it every morning to every week to once a month. At some point down the road you'll remember you're paying for something you don't need and don't use, and then you 'churn', even though the decision was made months ago.

If a user hasn't used your product in six months, they're at risk of churning. Or, if a user is exporting all of their data from their account, they might be salvaging what they can before canceling.

What causes activity churn? Maybe your customer forgot to cancel their subscription. Or the person who bought your product changed jobs. There are countless reasons, some of which are out of your control. But it'd be a shame not to *try* to prevent someone from cancelling their account, especially when you have that data at your fingertips.

(That said, you don't need to send a "We miss you" email to every user who goes a week without using your application. People take vacations. You don't want to smother users with annoying messages.)

How do you calculate activity churn? Unlike customer and revenue churn—where there's a simple formula—the formula for activity churn is unique to your product. It starts by measuring product engagement. Derek Skaletsky, CEO of Sherlock,[61] was kind enough to break down his five steps to tracking product engagement.

Step 1: Define Engagement for Your Product

Before you start, understand that your product is unique—and, therefore, defining engagement for your product will be different than for other products. Don't run away from this fact. Embrace it and create an engagement model based on important activities unique to your product.

For example, if you're a B2B productivity tool, you could define engagement as a certain number of "projects created," "tasks completed," "team members added," "comments left," "files uploaded," "projects completed," etc. A social networking application could define engagement as "connections made," "content posted," "posts liked," "comments made," etc.

The first step is to list engagement activities that a user can take in your product. For example:

- Logged in;

- Added photo;

- Shared photo;

- Invited friend;

- Commented on photo;

- Edited photo;

- Posted to Facebook;

- Posted to Twitter;

- Opened email;

- Clicked on email.

You'll iterate and refine these criteria over time as your product evolves, but once you have the list, you can move to Step 2.

Step 2: Start Tracking These Product Activities (i.e. Events)

I'm assuming most teams reading this are already tracking their important product events. But if you're not, what are you waiting for? Seriously, no excuses. Make it happen. I mean it. Why are you still reading this? Go! Get it done. Then move to Step 3.

Step 3: Weigh Each "Engagement" Event

Now that you're tracking your important engagement events, the next step is to weigh each event based on its impact, or its importance, to overall engagement with your product. This is an essential step—**not all activity is created equal.**

Think about it: Inviting a new user to your product is a more engaging act than simply logging in. Writing a long post on a social media site is more engaging than simply liking a post. Creating a project on a task management application is more engaging than simply completing a single task. And so on.

Weigh activities accordingly. Create a table that looks like the one below. List your engagement events on the left column and weigh each event on the right:

Event Name	Event Weight (between 1-10)
Event 1	3
Event 2	7
Event 3	9

Then, for each user, add a column for the number of times they triggered each event over a period of time (for example, the past seven days):

Event Name	Event Weight (between 1-10)	Number of Events (last X days)
Event 1	3	124
Event 2	7	23
Event 3	9	11

Next, simply multiply the event weight by the number of events. Your result should look something like this:

Event Name	Event Weight (between 1-10)	Number of Events (last X days)	Total Event Value (A*B)
Event 1	3	124	372
Event 2	7	23	161
Event 3	9	11	99
		TOTAL SCORE	632

The total for individual event values will give you an engagement score for an individual user. Finally, run this calculation for each user. You'll have the basis for a quantified user engagement score. But don't stop there. The next step is to give meaning to it all.

Step 4: Give It Context by Normalizing Raw Scores

If you're going through the exercise of creating an engagement score, it's essential that it's usable across your organization. This metric needs to be "operationalized" by your various teams. Your score needs to be in a format that's easily understood and consumed by anyone.

Simply telling your marketing team that a user has a score of 458 isn't helpful. How are they supposed to know if 458 is good or bad? Is that high or low? But telling them that a user has a score of 91 on a scale from 1 to 100 is something they can understand.

This is why you need to apply a normalization formula to your raw engagement scores. To normalize scores In Sherlock, they use a process called Winsorizing,[62] then apply an exponential function to ensure that differences in raw scores are represented effectively.

Step 5: Apply the Scores to Make Them Actionable

Once you normalize user scores, you've done the hard work. All that's left is using these scores in ways that have direct business applications. Here are a few ways to make this scoring model actionable:

1. Rank Your Users

When every user has an engagement score, you can do something amazing: actually rank users based on engagement. This opens up so many opportunities. For example, you can:

- Discover your power users and find out what makes them great.

- Prioritize customer-success efforts to drive great support, identify problem users, and spot growth opportunities.

- Drive more personalized marketing programs.

- Identify great user research targets.

This kind of user ranking can help you understand your users in the context of their actual engagement with your product—incredibly powerful!

2. Score and Rank Your Accounts

With all users scored for engagement, you can aggregate scores at the account level, which is essential for any SaaS business. As you can imagine, being able to rank your accounts will allow you to:

- Understand the overall health of your business.

- Prioritize sales efforts by knowing which trial or freemium accounts are more likely to convert.

- Prioritize customer-success efforts by focusing on accounts that are ripe for expansion and those that need support.

- Identify which features are most important to your best accounts.

3. Calculate the Overall Score for Your Product

By calculating a score for each one of your users, you can also aggregate those scores to create an engagement score for your product as a whole.

User	Engagement Score
User 1	188
User 2	12
User 3	45
TOTAL ENGAGEMENT	245
ENGAGEMENT/USER	82

By tracking this average score over time, you can determine whether the work you're doing on your product is actually driving engagement. You also might be able to make board-level decisions about when (or whether) to make further investments in the business.

4. Compare Populations or Cohorts

A user engagement metric is tremendously helpful when comparing different user populations. You can compare the engagement of new users vs. older users, users on a free plan vs. those on a paid plan, users with different access levels, etc. The opportunities are endless.

5. Correlate with Other Business Metrics

Product engagement is an essential metric for any software business. Ultimately, a good user engagement score isn't simply a valuable product metric—it's an essential business metric for any software business.

Comparing levels of user engagement to other business metrics like sales, retention, growth, LTV, etc., is a great way to forecast business progress based on engagement levels.

Once you measure product engagement, you can sniff out activity churn and combat it before it happens. Unlike customer and revenue churn—which look in the rear-view mirror—activity churn looks ahead and can save accounts before it's too late. In the next section, we'll cover some powerful tactics that can slay the churn beast.

Slaying the Churn Beast

Measure your churn metrics. As Peter Drucker, renowned management consultant, said, "If you can't measure it, you can't manage it." One of the main reasons that no one focuses on churn is that it's always seen as someone else's problem. As Kristen DeCosta of Churnbusters says, "If churn is everybody's job, then it's nobody's job."

Once someone in the company owns churn—and takes responsibility for measuring it and reporting it, you can move on to other tasks, like getting your customers started on the right foot.

Start customers off on the right foot. How common is it to sign up for a new product and have the only welcome email be a receipt confirming your purchase? For a lot of companies, this is the norm. They focus on creating an experience that converts you into a customer, but almost no thought goes into welcoming you as a customer and making sure you get value from the product.

A robust customer onboarding process is one of the most powerful ways to reduce churn. You can send customer welcome emails, have a dedicated 1:1 onboarding call, or send new customers incredible content to help them get value from your product. It's entirely up to you. Just make it a welcoming experience that gets users closer to their goals.

Conquer your ability debt. In Chapter 10, we talked about how ability debt is the price you pay every time your user can't accomplish a key outcome in your product. If your product is difficult to use, customers will churn because they can't experience the full value of your product. To chip away at your ability debt, you need to be ruthless about removing friction.

Send usage-review emails. Usage-review emails showcase the value of your product to your users. Mailchimp showcases emails sent. Wistia highlights who watched your videos and for how long. Fullstory delivers a daily or weekly log of the top users who interacted with your website.

Here's a usage-review email template from Userlist.io.[63] You can modify it for your business:

Usage Review Email

Subject: Your [Product] weekly activity report

Hi {{user.first_name | default: "there"}},

[Statement about what they accomplished with your product. E.g...

- Here's how many tasks your team accomplished last week

- Here's the current status of your proposals (drafted, sent, and accepted)

- Here's how many hours of work [Product] saved you last week]

[Activity section. Rule of thumb: only show activity that will make your user feel accomplished. A good barometer: is it activity they'd feel proud of, or want to show to their boss? If so, it's probably good activity to show. E.g...

- Number of new proposals sent

- Number of new proposals accepted

- Increased productivity

- Increased traffic

- Increased engagement with their content or product

- Increased sign-ups or revenue]

Happy [verb your product does]ing!

– Signature

Restate your value when invoicing. When you send invoices, remind people that they're paying for a product that they may or may not be using. If the latter, remind them why they signed up in the first place. Here's a great example from Zapier that reiterates the core benefits of their product:

Another Month of Automated Awesome

Hey Emil, we received your payment. Thanks for using Zapier to automate your workflows and save time!

With your **Professional Plus** plan, you can:

- ✅ Build workflows with 3+ steps
- ✅ Access premium-tier apps
- ✅ Use Autoreplay to protect against app downtime
- ✅ Run Zaps every 5 minutes

Your invoice for $125.00 is attached. Thanks again for using Zapier!

Your unique payment identifier is: in_Aaco5cFimONiSw

Your **Business Plus** plan was renamed **Professional Plus**, but everything else about it has remained the same.

Zapier knows that invoicing can trigger cancellations (especially if users are inactive), so they maximize every opportunity to reinforce the value their customers get from their product.

Create churn-prevention campaigns. Many SaaS companies spend thousands to acquire new customers. But when it comes to spending money to keep those same hard-earned customers, they won't open their wallets.

Churn-prevention campaigns could include a remarketing campaign to users with low activity, or booking 1:1 meetings with your customer success team. Get creative.

Have a robust cancellation process. Not knowing why your customers churned is a missed opportunity. Maybe users just didn't understand how to use your product. If that were the case, you could have reached out and offered a free onboarding call. To understand your churn, use a survey to collect data from recently cancelled accounts.

Your survey could be a single question: Why did you decide to cancel your account? It doesn't have to be complicated. Tie proactive action items to each potential response:

- Still evaluating → Offer a trial extension.

- Not a fit → Drop into a nurture funnel.

- Too complex → Schedule a customer success call.

- Too expensive → Provide a one-time discount.

- Went with another solution → Send top-of-funnel lead-nurturing emails to stay top-of-mind if other service doesn't work out.

This ensures you're constantly learning from churned customers and increasing your odds of winning them back.

Tackle delinquent churn. These are customers who churn after you're unable to bill

their credit cards. This can happen when a credit card expires and has to be updated. But it can also happen for a bunch of other reasons, such as insufficient funds or spending limits, and freezes for suspicious activity. According to ProfitWell, roughly 20–40% of MRR churn is due to failed credit cards. Putting a system in place to recover these customers can be incredibly valuable.

Invest in customer success. Many founders confuse "customer success" and "customer

support." Customer support is reactive and focused on answering tickets and fixing bugs. Customer success actively looks for ways to help customers succeed.

Fix your pricing. If you aren't using value metrics in your pricing model, your customers might churn because the value they're getting from your product is inadequate for the price. This can happen if you use arbitrary pricing levers, like charging by the user.

Now that you know some of the most powerful ways to reduce churn, improve your ARPU, and get more customers, it's time to put everything we learned into practice.

CHAPTER 16

Why Truly Great Companies Are Built to Be Product-Led

"Product-Led Growth will soon become the norm, making it table stakes for SaaS companies that want to win in their markets."

– Blake Bartlett, Partner, OpenView

What if Google required you to pay a fee before you could search for an answer to your problem? What if Uber said you needed to book a demo before your first ride? What if Slack required you to talk to sales before you could sign up?

What if the companies we welcome into our lives every single day didn't make it easy for us to experience the value of their product? Well, none of those companies would be as successful as they are. Giants like Google, Uber, and Slack have changed everything. The whole model for how businesses do business has changed, especially for B2B.

Today, choices are endless, and the buyer has all the control. As buyers, we're tired of jumping through hoops to get from Point A to Point B in a sales cycle. As Pete Caputa, CEO of Databox, puts it:

> The sales-led way of buying software: Read about the software, create a list of features needed, let sales qualify you, do a demo, and twist their arm so they give you a trial.
>
> The product-led way of buying software: Just start using the product. Ask for help if you get stuck. Based on your usage and profile, receive personalized recommendations.

Which sounds better to you? Whether you're selling perfume or software, trying out a product is and always will be an essential part of the buying process. Consumers demand it. Companies that embrace Product-Led Growth align their business model with an undeniable and enduring consumer trend.

History tells us that "how" you sell is just as important as "what" you sell. BlockBuster couldn't compete with Netflix by selling the same digital content. You, too, need to decide: Are you going to be product-led? Or will you risk being disrupted?

Thanks for Reading My Book!

By now, I'm sure you're well aware just how powerful Product-Led Growth can be for your business. But, for every one person, like you, who understands the power of Product-Led Growth, there are a thousand who have no idea what it's all about and how it can help them grow their business.

If you found this book helpful, I encourage you to share it with a friend, co-worker, or leave a review on Amazon so that others can find out what Product-Led Growth is all about.

Happy growing,

Wes Bush

Glossary

Product-Led Growth is a go-to-market strategy that relies on using your product as the main vehicle to acquire, activate, and retain customers.

Sales-Led GTM is when you rely on your sales team to close every single deal in your pipeline. You have no self-service offering.

Customer Acquisition Costs (CAC) is the cost of convincing a potential customer to buy a product or service.[64]

Revenue Per Employee (RPE) measures the average revenue generated by each employee of a company.[65]

A go-to-market (GTM) strategy is an action plan that specifies how a company will reach target customers and achieve a competitive advantage.[66]

Lifetime Value: (LTV) tells companies how much revenue they can expect one customer to generate over the course of the business relationship.[67]

Total addressable market: (TAM) is the overall revenue opportunity available or foreseen for a specific product or service, taking into account the future expansion scenarios.[68]

A **free trial** is a customer acquisition model that provides a partial or complete product to prospects free of charge for a limited time.

A **freemium model** is a customer acquisition model that provides access to part of a software product to prospects free of charge, without a time limit.

Dominant growth is when you can do something much better than your market *and* can charge significantly less.

Differentiated growth requires you to do a specific job better than the competition and charge significantly more. This is not a one-size-fits-all model.

Annual Contract Value (ACV) is the average annualized revenue per customer contract. It excludes any one time fees.[69]

Average revenue per user measures the amount of money that a company can expect to generate from an individual customer. It's calculated by dividing the total revenue of the business by its total number of users.[70]

Disruptive growth is when you charge less for what many might consider an "inferior product." Most people think this is a bad idea, but it's not.

Red Ocean companies try to outperform their rivals to grab a greater share of existing demand. As the market space gets crowded, prospects for profits and growth reduce. Products become commodities, and cut-throat competition turns the bloody ocean red.

Blue Ocean companies access untapped market space and create demand, and so they have the opportunity for highly profitable growth. In Blue Oceans, competition is irrelevant. Yes, imitators arise, but experience shows there is a wide window of opportunity to stay ahead of imitators.

Top-down selling is when your sales team targets key decision makers and executives. Typically, these deals include large product rollouts throughout an entire business.

Bottom-up selling is the norm in the consumer market. Take Facebook, Twitter, or Evernote: each created a product that can be adopted in minutes. Unlike the top-down selling strategy, where it might take months or years to close a sale (and another year to understand how to use the product), bottom-up selling strategies demand quick adoption and simplicity.

Value metric: A value metric is the way you measure value exchange in your product.

What we promise in our marketing and sales is the **per-**

ceived value.

What we deliver in our product is the **experienced value.**

Value Gap: If you fail to deliver, your user experiences a nasty value gap.

Ability debt is the price you pay every time your user fails to accomplish a key outcome in your product.

UCD framework stands for Understand, Communicate, and Deliver your value. Each element is a pillar in building a successful product-led foundation.

Functional Outcome: the core tasks that customers want to get done.

Emotional Outcome: how customers want to feel or avoid feeling as a result of executing the core functional outcome.

Social Outcome: how customers want to be perceived by others by using your product.

Best Judgement Pricing is when you and your team decide your price based on what you think would make a reasonable price.

Cost-Plus Pricing works when you calculate the cost of selling and delivering the product, then add a profit margin on top.

Competitor-based pricing is when you benchmark

your pricing off of your competitors.

Value-based pricing bases your price on the value you provide. You determine this by taking into account how prospects value your product.

Product bumpers are mission critical. They help users adopt the product within the application itself.

Conversational bumpers work to educate users, bring them back into the application, and eventually upgrade their account.

A **First-Run Onboarding Experience** is the first time a user goes through your onboarding experience.

References

1 Team, T. i. (2018, March 15). *How to build a SaaS with $0*. Retrieved from Hackernoon.

2 Chen, A. (n.d.). *Startups are cheaper to build, but more expensive to grow – here's why*. Retrieved from Andrew Chen.

3 Prater, J. (n.d.). *Facebook CPMs Increase 171% In 2017 [New Report]*. Retrieved from ADSTAGE.

4 Prater, J. (n.d.). *Twitter Ad Costs for 2017 [NEW REPORT]*. Retrieved from ADSTAGE.

5 Prater, J. (n.d.). *How Much Do LinkedIn Ads Cost? [New Report]*. Retrieved from ADSTAGE.

6 CAMPBELL, P. (n.d.). *INTERCOM'S DES TRAYNOR, STEVE BLANK ON HOW TO DO CUSTOMER RESEARCH*. Retrieved from ProfitWell.

7 Steven Casey, P. A. (2016, Feb 10). *How Self-Service Research Will Change B2B Marketing*. Retrieved from Forrester.

8 Aptrinsic. (2017, Oct 6). *CH 7: From a Traditional Go-To-Market to a Product-led Go-To-Market Strategy*. Retrieved from Intrinsicpoint.

9 Bush, W. (n.d.). *Free Trial vs Freemium: Use the MOAT Framework to Decide*. Retrieved from Traffic Is Currency.

10 PARTNERS, B. (n.d.). *GO-TO-MARKET STRATEGY*. Retrieved from BIN PARTNERS LLC.

11 Rajaram, G. (2018, April 19). *Self-serve first: the overlooked but essential paradigm underlying great software companies*. Retrieved from Medium Startups.

12 Rajaram, G. (2018, April 19). *Self-serve first: the overlooked but essential paradigm underlying great software companies*. Retrieved from Medium Startups.

13 Fanning, S. (2018, August 22). *PRODUCT LED GROWTH: THE SECRET TO BECOMING A TOP QUARTILE PUBLIC COMPANY*. Retrieved from Openview.

14 Ulwick, T. (2017, January 5). *The Jobs-to-be-Done Growth Strategy Matrix*. Retrieved from Jobs-to-be-Done.

15 Lemkin, J. (n.d.). *Why You Need 50 Million Active Users for Freemium to Actually Work*. Retrieved from SaaStr.

16 Kim, W. C. (2005, February 3). *Blue Ocean Strategy: How to Create Uncontested Market Space and Make Competition Irrelevant Hardcover*. Retrieved from Amazon.com.

17 BRIANNE. (2018, October 3). *Self-serve growth doesn't last forever, it's time to hire Sales*. Retrieved from BRIANNE KIMMEL.

18 CAMPBELL, P. (2019, May 4). *OUTCOME BASED VALUE METRICS DRIVE DOWN CHURN, INCREASE EXPANSION REVENUE*. Retrieved from ProfitWell.

19 Skok, D. (n.d.). *2016 Pacific Crest SaaS Survey – Part 1*. Retrieved from ForEntrepreneurs.

20 Intelligently, P. (n.d.). *The Anatomy of SaaS PRICING STRAT-EGY*. Retrieved from Price Intelligently.

21 Intelligently, P. (n.d.). *The Anatomy of SaaS PRICING STRAT-EGY*. Retrieved from Price Intelligently.

22 Intelligently, P. (n.d.). *The Anatomy of SaaS PRICING STRAT-EGY*. Retrieved from Price Intelligently.

23 Murphy, L. (n.d.). *SaaS Pricing Strategy: The 10x Rule*. Retrieved from Customer success-driven growth.

24 Funnelcake. (n.d.). *Sales accountability made easy*. Retrieved from Funnelcake.

25 Sam Nathan, K. S. (2013, October). *From Promotion to Emotion: Connecting B2B Customers to Brands*. Retrieved from Think Eith Google.

26 WOLF, T. (n.d.). *Emotional Targeting 101: How to Leverage the Power of Emotion to Grow Conversions*. Retrieved from GetUplift.

27 WOLF, T. (n.d.). *Emotional Targeting 101: How to Leverage the Power of Emotion to Grow Conversions*. Retrieved from GetUplift.

28 Murphy, L. (n.d.). *SaaS Pricing Strategy: The 10x Rule*. Retrieved from Customer success-driven growth.

29 QuestionPro. (2012, December 14). *How to Set Pricing Using the Van Westendorp Price Sensitivity Meter*. Retrieved from Slideshare.

30 Poyar, K. (2017). *MASTERING SAAS PRICING How to Price Your Product from the Seed Stage through IPO*. Retrieved from Open View.

31 Poyar, K. (2017). *MASTERING SAAS PRICING How to Price Your Product from the Seed Stage through IPO*. Retrieved from Open View.

32 Wesley Bush, m. s. (n.d.). *Grow your SaaS company faster through product-led growth strategy*. Retrieved from Conversionxl.

33 Curency, T. i. (n.d.). *SERVICES*. Retrieved from Traffic is curency.

34 Vidyard. (n.d.). *More than just video hosting*. Retrieved from vidyard.

35 Gorgias. (2019, February 22). *Lessons from Gorgias: How to Close your First 1000 Customers Based Solely on Data*. Retrieved from Youtube.

36 Doerr, J. (2018, April 24). *Measure What Matters: How Google, Bono, and the Gates Foundation Rock the World with OKRs*. Retrieved from Amazon.com.

37 Orston, R. (2018, April 12). *WHAT EVERY SAAS BUSINESS NEEDS TO KNOW ABOUT USER ADOPTION*. Retrieved from Openview.

38 Scott Williamson, V. o. (n.d.). *Input Log*. Retrieved from docs. google.com.

39 Mackin, Al, The Benefits of Showing Progress. Retrieved from Formisimo

40 HUANG, Y. Z.-C. (n.d.). *How Endowed versus Earned Progress Affects*. Retrieved from faculty.mccombs.utexas.edu.

41 Stretch, R. (2016, January 14). *The Endowed Progress Effect: How to Motivate Your Customers With a Head Start*. Retrieved from zapier.

42 Wikipedia. (2019, February 22). *Zeigarnik effect*. Retrieved from Wikipedia.

43 Wiebe, J. (n.d.). *We did these 7 things to a SaaS onboarding email sequence, and it tripled paid conversions*. Retrieved from Copyhackers.

44 ResultStory. (n.d.). *Your most powerful growth 'hack'*. Retrieved from ResultStory.

45 Bush, W. (n.d.). *Little Known Ways To Convert Free Trial Users Into Premium Customers*. Retrieved from Traffic Is Currency.

46 Bush, W. (n.d.). *Free Trial vs Freemium: Use the MOAT Framework to Decide*. Retrieved from Traffic Is Currency.

47 Dimon, G. (2016, October 20). *Ttrial expiration email best practices*. Retrieved from Postmark.

48 Geary, M. (2018, November 14). *The marketer's guide to conversion rate optimization*. Retrieved from Autopilot.

49 EXPERT, M. (2017, February 22). *Returning Customers Spend 67% More Than New Customers - Keep Your Customers Coming Back with a Recurring Revenue Sales Model*. Retrieved from Business.com.

50 CAMPBELL, P. (2017, May 21). *BRIAN BALFOUR: WHY SAAS COMPANIES ARE WRONG ABOUT PRODUCT-MARKET FIT*. Retrieved from Priceintelligently.

51 Schwartz, B. (n.d.). *The Paradox of Choice: Why More Is Less MP3 CD – Audiobook, MP3 Audio, Unabridged*. Retrieved from Amazon.com.

52 CAMPBELL, P. (2017, May 21). *HOW TO TURN A SAAS COMPANY AROUND IN 90 DAYS [CASE STUDY]*. Retrieved from Priceintelligently.

53 Smith, R. F. (n.d.). *Robert F. Smith*. Retrieved from Forbes.

54 Olende, R. O. (n.d.). *Roy Opata Olende*. Retrieved from Twitter.

55 Reichheld, F. (n.d.). *Prescription for cutting costs*. Retrieved from Bain & Company.

56 CAMPBELL, P. (2017, April 14). *DATA SHOWS OUR AD-DICTION TO ACQUISITION BASED GROWTH IS GET-TING WORSE.* Retrieved from Priceintelligently.

57 TATE, A. (2019, May 06). *HOW TO REDUCE CHURN BY BUILDING A BULLETPROOF RETENTION PROCESS.* Retrieved from Profitwell.

58 BRIANNE. (2018, October 3). *Self-serve growth doesn't last forever, it's time to hire Sales.* Retrieved from BRIANNE KIMMEL.

59 BRIANNE. (2018, October 3). *Self-serve growth doesn't last forever, it's time to hire Sales.* Retrieved from BRIANNE KIMMEL.

60 Traynor, D. (n.d.). *Reduce churn by re-engaging your customers.* Retrieved from Intercom.

61 Sherlock. (n.d.). *The game of SaaS is afoot! Are you ready to start winning?* Retrieved from Sherlock.

62 Wikipedia. (n.d.). *Winsorizing.* Retrieved from Wikipedia.

63 Userlist. (n.d.). *Send the Right Message at the Right Time.* Retrieved from userlist.

64 Neilpatel. (n.d.). *Customer Acquisition Cost: The One Metric That Can Determine Your Company's Fate.* Retrieved from Neilpatel.

65 Investinganswers. (n.d.). *Revenue Per Employee.* Retrieved from Investinganswers.

66 PARTNERS, B. (n.d.). *GO-TO-MARKET STRATEGY.* Retrieved from BIN PARTNERS LLC.

67 Fontanella, C. (n.d.). *How to Calculate Customer Lifetime Value.* Retrieved from blog.hubspot.com.

68 Divestopedia. (n.d.). *Total Addressable Market (TAM).* Retrieved from Divestopedia.

69 Baremetrics. (n.d.). *Annual Contract Value (ACV)*. Retrieved from Baremetrics.

70 Farley, R. (n.d.). *ARPU: How to Calculate and Interpret Average Revenue Per User*. Retrieved from blog.hubspot.com.

Made in the USA
Las Vegas, NV
26 December 2023

83503529R00163